OFFICIAL
SQA
PAST
PAPERS
WITH ANSWERS

HIGHER

PHYSICAL EDUCATION
2007-2011

Publisher's Note

We are delighted to bring you the 2011 Past Papers and you will see that we have changed the format from previous editions. As part of our environmental awareness strategy, we have attempted to make these new editions as sustainable as possible.

To do this, we have printed on white paper and bound the answer sections into the book. This not only allows us to use significantly less paper but we are also, for the first time, able to source all the materials from sustainable sources.

We hope you like the new editions and by purchasing this product, you are not only supporting an independent Scottish publishing company but you are also, in the International Year of Forests, not contributing to the destruction of the world's forests.

Thank you for your support and please see the following websites for more information to support the above statement –

www.fsc-uk.org

www.loveforests.com

First exam published in 2007.
Published by Bright Red Publishing Ltd, 6 Stafford Street, Edinburgh EH3 7AU
tel: 0131 220 5804 fax: 0131 220 6710 info@brightredpublishing.co.uk www.brightredpublishing.co.uk

ISBN 978-1-84948-223-3

A CIP Catalogue record for this book is available from the British Library.

Bright Red Publishing is grateful to the copyright holders, as credited on the final page of the Question Section, for permission to use their material. Every effort has been made to trace the copyright holders and to obtain their permission for the use of copyright material. Bright Red Publishing will be happy to receive information allowing us to rectify any error or omission in future editions.

HIGHER

2007

[BLANK PAGE]

X205/301

NATIONAL
QUALIFICATIONS
2007

FRIDAY, 25 MAY
9.00 AM – 11.30 AM

PHYSICAL
EDUCATION
HIGHER

Candidates should attempt **three** questions, each chosen from a different area.

SCOTTISH
QUALIFICATIONS
AUTHORITY

©

AREA 1: PERFORMANCE APPRECIATION

Marks

Question 1

Choose an activity.

(a) Describe the **nature** and **demands** of a quality performance within your selected activity.

6

(b) Mental factors can influence your performance. Explain how you were able to manage your emotions and mental state for a performance in your selected activity.

4

(c) When planning for performance improvement, discuss why it is important to use an **integrated training** (combination) approach to develop your whole performance. Give examples from your training programme to support your answer.

6

(d) Discuss why it is important to **monitor** and **review** your performance development.

4

(20)

Question 2

Choose an activity.

(a) Discuss the **positive** and **negative** influence of mental factors on performance.

4

(b) Technical, physical, personal and special qualities are important when performing. Select **three** of these qualities and explain their importance.

6

(c) Describe, in detail, the **strengths** and **weaknesses** in your whole performance in relation to **one** of the qualities you selected within part (b).

4

(d) Explain how you organised your training to **improve your weaknesses** whilst **maintaining your strengths**. Give examples from your training to support your answer.

6

(20)

AREA 2: PREPARATION OF THE BODY

Marks

Question 3

Choose an activity.

(a) Describe in detail the **range** of fitness requirements for effective performance.

6

(b) Discuss why it is important to gather information about your **fitness**.

4

(c) Training can take place:

- **within the activity (conditioning)**
- **outwith the activity**
- **through a combination of both.**

Select **one** of the above and briefly outline a training programme. Discuss why it was appropriate for you to train using the selected approach.

6

(d) Having monitored your level of fitness during your training programme you will have made changes. Explain why these changes were necessary. Give examples to support your answer.

4

(20)

Question 4

Choose an activity.

(a) Select an aspect of **skill related** fitness. Describe **one** method of gathering information on this aspect. Explain why this method was appropriate.

4

(b) Explain the importance of **mental** fitness within an activity of your choice.

4

(c) Discuss the importance of **setting goals** to improve your level of **physical** fitness. Give examples of the goals you set.

6

(d) Discuss how you **planned** and **implemented** a training programme to achieve the goals set in part (c).

6

(20)

[Turn over

AREA 3: SKILLS AND TECHNIQUES

Marks

Question 5

Choose an activity and a skill or technique.

(a) When learning and developing a skill, it is important to work through the three stages of learning. These are:

- **the preparation/cognitive stage**
- **the practice/associative stage**
- **the automatic/autonomous stage.**

Explain what you understand about **each** stage.   **6**

(b) Discuss why it is appropriate to use different methods of practice at **two different** stages of learning. Give examples from your programme of work to support your answer.   **6**

(c) Describe how you monitored your progress as you worked through your development programme.   **4**

(d) Having developed this skill/technique, discuss the **effect** that this has had on your **whole** performance.   **4**

    (20)

Question 6

Choose an activity and a skill or technique.

(a) Describe the **features** of a skilled performance in this activity.   **4**

(b) When learning or developing a skill or technique, discuss the importance of **one** of the following:

- (i) **Information Processing Model**
- (ii) **Skill classification**.   **4**

(c) Describe, in detail, the **methods** you used to gather information on your level of performance. Explain why these methods were appropriate.   **6**

(d) From the information gathered, briefly describe a programme of work you used to develop this skill or technique. Explain why it is important to **review** your programme.   **6**

    (20)

AREA 4: STRUCTURES, STRATEGIES AND COMPOSITION *Marks*

Question 7

Choose an activity and a Structure, Strategy or Composition.

(a) Discuss why it is important to gather information about your performance when applying the Structure, Strategy or Composition. Give examples of the strengths and weaknesses you identified. **6**

(b) Describe how you addressed the weaknesses highlighted in part (a). Explain the actions you took. **4**

(c) When addressing your weaknesses you will have monitored your progress. Explain why this process is important. **4**

(d) Structures, Strategies or Compositions are based on a number of key principles/fundamentals. For example:

- **speed in attack**
- **width/depth/mobility**
- **using repetition, variation and contrast**
- **the importance of creativity.**

Choose **two**, **either from your course or** from the list above and explain their importance when applying the Structure, Strategy or Composition. **6**

(20)

Question 8

Choose an activity.

(a) Describe, in **detail**, a Structure, Strategy or Composition you have used. **4**

(b) Discuss some of the **problems** that **either** you **or** your team/group experienced when applying this Structure, Strategy or Composition. **6**

(c) With reference to the problems you experienced in part (b), discuss the **decisions** you took to develop and improve your performance. **6**

(d) Explain how you evaluated any improvements that were made in your performance in the chosen Structure, Strategy or Composition. **4**

(20)

[END OF QUESTION PAPER]

[BLANK PAGE]

HIGHER

2008

[BLANK PAGE]

X205/301

| NATIONAL QUALIFICATIONS 2008 | WEDNESDAY, 28 MAY 9.00 AM – 11.30 AM | PHYSICAL EDUCATION HIGHER |

Candidates should attempt **three** questions, each chosen from a different area.

AREA 1: PERFORMANCE APPRECIATION

Marks

Question 1

Choose an activity.

(a) Describe in detail your personal performance in relation to **two** of the performance qualities listed below.

- **Technical**
- **Physical**
- **Personal**
- **Special**

6

(b) Select **one** of the qualities highlighted in Part (a). Describe in detail how you gathered information about this quality during your **overall** performance.

4

(c) Why is it important to use appropriate models of performance when developing your own performance?

4

(d) Discuss the importance of goal setting when planning your performance development. Give specific examples of the goals you set.

6

(20)

Question 2

Choose an activity.

(a) Explain what you understand about the **mental factors** which affect performance.

4

(b) Select a mental factor that had a negative effect on your performance. What method(s) did you use to overcome this difficulty? Why was the method(s) appropriate?

6

(c) Select a **weakness** within your whole performance. Discuss how you planned and managed a programme of improvement to develop your performance.

6

(d) Explain why it is important to review the effectiveness of your programme of improvement.

4

(20)

AREA 2: PREPARATION OF THE BODY

Marks

Question 3

Choose an activity.

(a) Describe the physical, skill related and mental fitness requirements for effective performance within your activity. **6**

(b) From the fitness requirements described in Part (a), select **one** aspect. Explain how you gathered information about it **within** the activity. **4**

(c) There are three phases of training:

- **preparation** (pre season)
- **competition** (during the season)
- **transition** (off season).

Discuss why your training might differ between **each** of the phases. Give examples to support your answer. **6**

(d) Describe **one** method of training you used to develop your fitness. Explain why this method was appropriate. **4**

(20)

Question 4

(a) Describe in detail a situation where your level of fitness:

(i) was a **strength** to your performance;

(ii) was a **weakness** to your performance.

(You may wish to answer this question through more than one activity.) **6**

(b) With reference to either the strength or weakness identified in Part (a), describe in detail **one** method of training you used to develop your fitness. **4**

(c) Discuss the **principles of training** you would consider when designing and completing a training programme. **6**

(d) Explain why it is important to evaluate the effectiveness of your training programme. **4**

(20)

[Turn over

AREA 3: SKILLS AND TECHNIQUES

Marks

Question 5

(a) Select **two** of the influential factors listed below.

   - **Motivation**
   - **Concentration**
   - **Feedback**

   Explain what you understand about each factor.   **6**

   Choose an activity and a skill or technique.

(b) Describe the programme of work that you followed to develop this skill or technique.   **4**

(c) Discuss how the **principles of effective practice** were applied to the programme.   **6**

(d) Explain how your whole performance was affected on completion of this programme of work.   **4**

(20)

Question 6

Choose an activity and a skill or technique.

(a) Select **one** of the following approaches. Describe how you gathered information about your chosen skill or technique using this approach.

   - **Mechanical analysis**
   - **Movement analysis**
   - **Consideration of quality**   **4**

(b) Discuss the results of the information gathered in Part (a). Make specific reference to how your **whole** performance was affected.   **6**

(c) Outline the programme of work that you followed to develop your performance in this skill or technique. Explain why this programme of work was appropriate.   **6**

(d) Explain why it is important to monitor and review your programme of work.   **4**

(20)

AREA 4: STRUCTURES, STRATEGIES AND COMPOSITION

Marks

Question 7

Choose an activity.

(*a*) Describe a Structure, Strategy or Composition that you have used. What were your strength(s) when applying this Structure, Strategy or Composition? **6**

(*b*) Discuss how you planned your performance to make best use of your strength(s) when performing in this Structure, Strategy or Composition. **4**

(*c*) Describe your weakness(es) when applying this Structure, Strategy or Composition. Discuss the effect that this had on your performance. **6**

(*d*) Explain what you did to reduce the effect of the weakness(es) identified. **4**

(20)

Question 8

Choose an activity.

(*a*) Discuss the factors that you would take into consideration when selecting a Structure, Strategy or Composition. **6**

(*b*) Describe in detail a Structure, Strategy or Composition that you have used. **4**

(*c*) Briefly describe a situation where you had to **adapt or change** the Structure, Strategy or Composition in Part (*b*). Discuss why these changes or adaptations made your performance more effective. **6**

(*d*) Having adapted or changed this Structure, Strategy or Composition, explain how you would evaluate its effectiveness. **4**

(20)

[END OF QUESTION PAPER]

[BLANK PAGE]

2009

[BLANK PAGE]

X205/301

NATIONAL QUALIFICATIONS 2009	MONDAY, 1 JUNE 9.00 AM – 11.30 AM	PHYSICAL EDUCATION HIGHER

Candidates should attempt **three** questions, each chosen from a different area.

AREA 1: PERFORMANCE APPRECIATION

Marks

Question 1

Choose an activity.

(a) What do you understand about the **demands** of a quality performance in your chosen activity? **4**

(b) Describe your performance in comparison to a quality performance in your chosen activity. **6**

(c) Discuss a training programme you followed that took into account your strengths and any development needs you may have. **6**

(d) Describe how you monitored the effectiveness of this training programme. **4**

(20)

Question 2

Choose an activity.

(a) How can the study of model performance help you in your chosen activity? **4**

(b) Describe

  (i) your strengths

  (ii) your weaknesses

in comparison to a model performance in your chosen activity. **6**

(c) What course of action would you take to improve your performance? Explain your reasons for this course of action. **6**

(d) Why is it important to evaluate the effects of this course of action on your whole performance? **4**

(20)

AREA 2: PREPARATION OF THE BODY

Marks

Question 3

Choose an activity.

(*a*) Select an aspect of fitness. Describe how you assessed this aspect of fitness both **within** and **outwith** your chosen activity.   **6**

(*b*) Why is it important to assess your fitness? Justify your reasons.   **4**

(*c*) What do you understand about the principles of training? Give examples of how these were used within your training programme.   **6**

(*d*) What impact did your training have on your whole performance? Give examples to support your answer.   **4**

(20)

Question 4

Choose an activity.

(*a*) Describe one skill related and one physical aspect of fitness required for effective performance in your chosen activity.   **4**

(*b*) Select **one** method of training you have used to develop a physical aspect of fitness.

Describe what you did when using this method. Discuss the **advantages** of using the method.   **6**

(*c*) Select **a different** method of training you have used to develop a skill related aspect of fitness.

Describe what you did when using this method. Discuss the **advantages** of using the method.   **6**

(*d*) Why is it important to monitor and review your programme of work?   **4**

(20)

[Turn over

AREA 3: SKILLS AND TECHNIQUES

Marks

Question 5

Choose an activity.

(a) Describe **two** methods you used to gather information on your performance.   **4**

(b) Describe, briefly, **one** skill or technique which is a **strength** in your performance and **one** skill or technique which is a **weakness**.   **4**

(c) Discuss how you planned a **progressive** improvement programme to address the weakness identified in part (b). Give examples from this programme to support your answer.   **6**

(d) Discuss the success of this programme on your whole performance. Why may there still be weakness(es) in your whole performance?   **6**

(20)

Question 6

Choose an activity.

(a) From analysis of your whole performance, describe your development needs.   **4**

(b) Describe two **methods of practice** you used to improve your development needs. Explain why each method was appropriate.   **6**

(c) What do you understand about the principles of effective practice? Give examples of how these were used within your programme.   **6**

(d) Explain why it is important to monitor your training programme.   **4**

(20)

AREA 4: STRUCTURES, STRATEGIES AND COMPOSITION

Marks

Question 7

Choose an activity.

(a) Describe the role you played **or** the performance you gave within a structure, strategy or composition you have used.

4

(b) Discuss the strengths required to carry out this role or performance effectively.

6

(c) Describe the programme of work you went through to develop the role you played or the performance you gave as identified in part (a).

6

(d) Explain why it is important to review your programme of work.

4

(20)

Question 8

(a) Select **one** of the following and explain its importance when planning a structure, strategy or composition.

- **Individual strengths and weaknesses**
- **Need to cooperate and support others in a team or group situation**
- **Identifying and exploiting opponents' weaknesses**
- **Timing, precision and improvisation in performance**

4

Choose an activity.

(b) Describe, briefly, a structure, strategy or composition you have used. Explain the advantages of using this structure, strategy or composition in your performance.

6

(c) Describe, briefly, the weakness(es) you found when carrying out your structure, strategy or composition. Justify the course of action you took to minimise the effects of this weakness(es).

6

(d) What improvements can now be observed in your whole performance?

4

(20)

[END OF QUESTION PAPER]

[BLANK PAGE]

[BLANK PAGE]

X205/301

| NATIONAL QUALIFICATIONS 2010 | TUESDAY, 1 JUNE 9.00 AM – 11.30 AM | PHYSICAL EDUCATION HIGHER |

Candidates should attempt **three** questions, each chosen from a different area.

AREA 1: PERFORMANCE APPRECIATION

Marks

Question 1

Choose an activity.

(*a*) Quality performance depends on:

- fluency
- economy of effort
- precision
- accuracy
- control.

Select **two** of the above and explain the importance of each.

6

(*b*) Why is it important to use an **integrated (combination) training approach** to develop whole performance? Justify your answer by giving examples from your programme.

4

(*c*) Discuss the importance of using short and long term goals. Give examples to support your answer.

6

(*d*) Describe the methods used to evaluate the success of the programme in achieving your goals.

4

(20)

Question 2

(*a*) Discuss the importance of considering models of performance when establishing training priorities.

4

Choose an activity.

(*b*) Describe the **nature** and **demands** of this activity.

6

(*c*) Describe your initial level of performance with reference to technical, physical, personal and special qualities.

4

(*d*) Select one of the qualities from part (*c*).

Discuss how a programme of work helped you to improve your overall level of performance. Give examples to support your answer.

6

(20)

AREA 2: PREPARATION OF THE BODY *Marks*

Question 3

    (*a*) Discuss why it is appropriate to train using each of the following approaches.

         • Within the activity (conditioning)
         • Outwith the activity
         • Through a combination of both   **6**

Choose an activity.

    (*b*) Explain how you planned and implemented your training programme.   **6**

    (*c*) Describe **one** training session that you undertook to develop your personal level of performance.   **4**

    (*d*) How did you monitor your progress within the training programme?   **4**

        (20)

Question 4

Choose an activity.

    (*a*) Explain the importance of each of the following types of fitness in your chosen activity.

         • Physical
         • Skill-related
         • Mental   **6**

    (*b*) Select **one** aspect of fitness.

        Describe **one** method you used to gather information on this aspect.   **4**

    (*c*) Explain why the method used was both **valid** and **reliable.**   **4**

    (*d*) Describe, briefly, one method of training to improve your performance in this activity. Discuss why this method was appropriate.   **6**

        (20)

[Turn over

AREA 3: SKILLS AND TECHNIQUES   *Marks*

Question 5

(*a*) Explain what you understand about the following.

- Information Processing model
- Skill classification   **6**

Choose an activity.

(*b*) Compare your whole performance to that of a model performance.   **4**

Select a skill or technique.

(*c*) Describe, in detail, the different methods of practice you used to develop this skill or technique.   **6**

(*d*) Discuss why it is important to monitor and review your development programme.   **4**

                                                                            (20)

Question 6

(*a*) Explain what you understand about the stages of learning.   **6**

Choose an activity and a skill or technique.

(*b*) For one stage of learning, select a method of practice you used to develop this skill or technique. Explain why this method was appropriate.   **4**

(*c*) Select **two** of the following.

- Motivation
- Concentration
- Feedback

Discuss the importance of **both** when carrying out your development programme.   **6**

(*d*) Having developed this skill or technique, describe the effect this had on your whole performance.   **4**

                                                                            (20)

AREA 4: STRUCTURES, STRATEGIES AND COMPOSITION   *Marks*

Question 7

Choose an activity.

(*a*) Describe a structure, strategy or composition you have used.   **4**

(*b*) What factors did you take into consideration when selecting this structure, strategy or composition?   **4**

(*c*) Describe briefly a situation where this structure, strategy or composition was not effective. Explain why this was the case in this situation.   **6**

(*d*) What changes/adaptations did you make to address this situation? Justify the actions that were taken.   **6**

                    (20)

Question 8

Choose an activity and structure, strategy or composition.

(*a*) (i) Describe **one** strength when performing in this structure, strategy or composition. Explain the effects this had on your performance.   **3**

    (ii) Describe **one** weakness when performing in this structure, strategy or composition. Explain the effects this had on your performance.   **3**

(*b*) Explain what you did to address the weakness identified in part (*a*) (ii).   **4**

(*c*) Describe how you evaluated the effectiveness of your performance in relation to the weakness identified in part (*a*) (ii).   **4**

(*d*) The following are key fundamentals when applying a structure, strategy or composition.

- Using space effectively in performance
- Using repetition, variation and contrast in performance
- Using creativity
- Width, depth and mobility

Select **two** of the above and explain the importance of each when applying your chosen structure, strategy or composition.   **6**

                    (20)

[END OF QUESTION PAPER]

[BLANK PAGE]

[BLANK PAGE]

X205/301

NATIONAL
QUALIFICATIONS
2011

MONDAY, 30 MAY
9.00 AM – 11.30 AM

PHYSICAL
EDUCATION
HIGHER

Candidates should attempt **three** questions, each chosen from a different area.

Marks

AREA 1: PERFORMANCE APPRECIATION

Question 1

Choose an activity.

(*a*) Discuss how your **overall** performance compares to that of a model performance.   **6**

(*b*) Select **one** of the following performance qualities.

- Technical
- Physical
- Personal
- Special

Describe a programme of work you followed to improve this quality.   **4**

(*c*) How did you make the most of your strengths within this quality when performing?   **4**

(*d*) Why is it important to evaluate your overall performance following the programme of work described in part (*b*)? Describe how this evaluation was carried out.   **6**

(20)

Question 2

Choose an activity.

(*a*) Describe the **nature** of a quality performance in this activity.   **4**

(*b*) How did you prepare mentally for this quality performance?   **4**

(*c*) Describe, in detail, an **integrated** (combination) improvement programme that developed your performance.   **6**

(*d*) Discuss the improvements in your overall performance following this improvement programme.   **6**

(20)

Marks

AREA 2: PREPARATION OF THE BODY

Question 3

Choose an activity.

(a) Why is it important to gather information about your fitness **before** carrying out a training programme?   **4**

(b) Explain what you understand about the three phases of training.   **6**

(c) Select **one** phase of training. Describe a training programme you used to develop or maintain your fitness during this phase.   **4**

(d) Throughout the different phases of your training you will have set personal goals. Give examples of the goals you set.

Discuss the factors you considered when setting these goals.   **6**

(20)

Question 4

(a) Explain the importance of mental aspects of fitness to performance.   **4**

Choose an activity.

(b) Describe, in detail, the physical and skill-related aspects of fitness required for this activity.   **6**

(c) Discuss the principles of training you considered when planning a fitness programme.   **6**

(d) During your training programme you will have made changes. Explain why these changes were necessary.   **4**

(20)

[Turn over

Marks

AREA 3: SKILLS AND TECHNIQUES

Question 5

Choose an activity.

(a) Describe the information you gathered about your performance using **one** of the following approaches.

- Mechanical Analysis
- Movement Analysis
- Consideration of quality   **4**

(b) Explain why you considered this approach to be appropriate.   **4**

(c) Justify the course of action you took to improve your performance.   **6**

(d) Explain the importance of using different types of feedback when developing performance.   **6**

(20)

Question 6

(a) Explain the advantages of considering a model performance when developing performance.   **4**

Choose an activity and a skill or technique.

(b) Describe the strengths and/or weaknesses you found when applying this skill or technique.   **4**

(c) Discuss the **principles of effective practice** you considered when planning your development programme.   **6**

(d) Describe **one** method of practice you used to improve your performance.

Explain why this method was relevant.   **6**

(20)

Marks

AREA 4: STRUCTURES, STRATEGIES AND COMPOSITION

Question 7

Choose an activity and a structure, strategy or composition.

(a) Describe how you gathered information about your performance when applying this structure, strategy or composition.   **4**

(b) Explain why this structure, strategy or composition makes the best use of your performance strengths.   **6**

(c) Describe the problems you encountered when applying this structure, strategy or composition.   **4**

(d) Justify the decisions you took to develop your performance within this structure, strategy or composition.   **6**

(20)

Question 8

Choose an activity.

(a) Describe **two different** structures, strategies or compositions you have used in this activity.   **6**

(b) Select **one** of these structures, strategies or compositions.
Explain the advantage(s) of using it in a performance situation.   **4**

(c) Explain the advantage(s) of using the **other** structure, strategy or composition in a performance situation.   **4**

(d) Discuss **one limitation of each** of these structures, strategies or compositions.   **6**

(20)

[END OF QUESTION PAPER]

[BLANK PAGE]

HIGHER | ANSWER SECTION

HIGHER PHYSICAL EDUCATION 2007

In the Higher Physical Education examination candidates will answer from the perspective of their experiences in a wide variety of activities. An activity specific answer section would result in an enormous document which would be extremely cumbersome and time-consuming to use and which could never realistically cover all possibilities.

In relation to **all** questions it should be noted that the relevance of the content in the candidates' responses will depend on:

- the activity selected
- the performance focus
- the training/development programme/programme of work selected
- the practical experiences of their course as the contexts for answers.

PERFORMANCE APPRECIATION

1. (a) *A good response should include some or most of the points as outlined below. The candidate's answer should include detail with relevant examples to support acquired Knowledge and Understanding.*

   #### Nature and Demands

   Nature: Individual/team. The duration of the game/event. The number of player(s)/performers involved. A spectator/audience event. Indoor/outdoor. Directly/indirectly competitive. Objective/subjective scoring systems in application. Codes of conduct.

   Demands: Technical, Physical, Mental and Special. Candidates may demonstrate acquired Knowledge and Understanding across all related demands or focus on one more comprehensively. Similarly, candidates may demonstrate acquired Knowledge and Understanding in respect of the unique game/event demands or emphasise the demands unique to the role/solo/duo performance relative to the activity selected.

   Special Performance Qualities: The responses will be wide ranging and relevant to the activity selected. Candidates may demonstrate acquired Knowledge and Understanding in respect of the specific role/solo related demands necessary for an effective performance.

   Reference to the application of a series of complex skills will impact on performance in competitive situations. For example: in relation to **role demands**,... *as a central defender I am pushed to my limits in the later stages of the game... it is essential that I time my tackles or I will give away penalties... I need to control the ball artistically to wrong foot my opponent and get the ball out of danger areas... etc*

   in relation to **solo demands**... *as a gymnast I know that my tumbling routine has many complex skills that need to be performed in a linked sequence... I need tremendous focus as often I will be pushing myself to the limits... etc... most importantly I need to add flair and fluency in my routine to attract the best marks from the judges... etc.*

   Candidates who are elite performers may demonstrate acquired Knowledge and Understanding in respect of the application of strategy/composition at appropriate times to ensure an effective performance. Often this link is made in cognisance of Knowledge of Performance and/or Knowledge of Results. For example: *reflecting on previous performances we knew to double mark their Knowledge and Understanding player as this would... etc... by applying a man to man strategy immediately would effectively tire them out and give us an advantage... etc... reflecting on my previous results I had to decide which solo piece to execute that would attract the best marks from the judges... etc.*

   (b) *A good response should include some or most of the points as outlined below. The candidate's answer should include full detail with relevant examples to support Knowledge and Understanding.*

   Mental factors: A good response will show Knowledge and Understanding by referring to the ability to manage emotions, deal with cognitive/somatic anxiety, level of arousal whether over or under, or handling stress affected by self confidence, motivation/concentration. *In the explanation given, reference may be made to deep breathing exercises or self talk or picturing the performance in your mind.*

   Reference may be made to the potential *effects* of positive and negative mental factors on performance and/or the internal/intrinsic, external/extrinsic effects.

   For example, *a positive influence* will impact upon performance by increasing state of mind/state of arousal and so enable the performer to produce sound levels of effectiveness/perform at maximum potential level/handle the pressure and remain calm/make appropriate decisions and enable appropriate actions in response to the immediate situation. There may be heightened awareness/confidence/early preparedness/few unforced errors/sustained performance standards and production of consistent application of skills to deal with the performance context. Reference may also be made to Knowledge of Performance/Knowledge of Results or external factors such as crowd, level of competition and rewards.

   Conversely – *a negative influence* will impact upon performance producing an ineffective/erratic and unconfident performance; cognitive anxiety - apprehension before and during performance, nerves get the better; somatic anxiety – physiological response, and so more unforced errors/fouls/made, severe lapse of concentration which may cause poor decision making or an inability to stick to role related duties associated with application of structure/strategy, etc.

   (c) *A good response should include some or most of the points as outlined below. The candidate's answer should include detail with relevant examples to support applied Knowledge and Understanding.*

   #### The importance of integrated training

   Typically the notion of more than one type of fitness/demand being developed at the same time. Reasons should be included to exhibit related Knowledge and Understanding.

   The training programme offered may reflect the development of a technical and skill related quality/demand being developed (or any other relevant combinations). For example, in badminton: *my aim was to develop the drop shot WHILST developing improved footwork (agility)*. The response should include relevant facts; *train in the activity using repetition drills/moving to take feeds from right and left hand side of court/combine with footwork drill, eg from T to various numbered areas of court. Progress to combination/ conditioned rallies to ensure refinement of shot ie efficiency, accuracy and disguised placement as a result of energy efficient movement to meet the shot with balance and poise to execute the shot and return to base ready for the next shot etc.*

A good response will typically include other relevant factors to demonstrate Knowledge and Understanding such as, progression, model performers, feedback, target setting, work to rest considerations, Stages of Learning, complexity of technique being developed, factors affecting performance, principles of training and or effective practice.

(d) *A good response should include some or most of the points as outlined below. The candidate's answer should include detailed discussion to demonstrate the difference between monitoring and reviewing.*

The importance of monitoring and reviewing

A good response will highlight the differences/ benefits of the purpose of monitoring = ongoing process. Such as reference to appropriate data methods to facilitate comparison of improvements, achieving targets set, gaining and acting on feedback, aids motivation, ensures further challenge and progress.

Importantly, the response must include reference to reviewing performance = summative progress. The structure of the question may enable the candidate to offer a 'holistic' overview – this is deemed acceptable.

Many candidates will repeat or include some of the previously mentioned comments. However reference to the evaluation of the **whole** process ie the impact of the training/development programme/programme of work should be highlighted. Judgements on the success/ effectiveness of the programme/used **plus** judgements on the success/effectiveness to whole performance must be clearly defined.

2. (a) *A good response should include some or most of the points as outlined below. The candidate's answer should include full detail with relevant examples to demonstrate acquired Knowledge and Understanding. This answer must display both positive and negative elements.*

Positive and Negative influences of mental factors

A good response will highlight the potential effects that positive and negative mental factors impact performance.

For example, *a positive influence* will impact upon performance by increasing state of mind/state of arousal and so enable the performer to produce sound levels of effectiveness/perform at maximum potential level/handle the pressure and remain calm/make appropriate decisions and enable appropriate actions in response to the immediate situation. There may be heightened awareness/confidence/ early preparedness/few unforced errors/sustained performance standards and production of consistent application of skills to deal with the performance context. Reference may also be made to external factors such as crowd, level of competition and rewards.

Conversely – *a negative influence* will impact upon performance in producing an ineffective/erratic/and unconfident performance. Other points raised may include apprehension/suffering cognitive and or somatic anxiety/the feeling of defeat before the event has begun etc.

A link to other relevant factors may include; bad temper, nervousness/lack of commitment/committing fouls, over confidence/lacking confidence etc.

(b) *A good response should include some or most of the points as outlined below. The candidate's answer should include full detail with relevant examples to demonstrate acquired Knowledge and Understanding in the related areas of three of the following: technical, physical, personal and special qualities.*

Qualities: In relation to **any** of the qualities selected a detailed personal description should be offered. In this respect the candidate may elect to answer from the viewpoint of having a positive or negative effect on performance. Similarly the description could be offered *via* a synopsis of strengths and weaknesses **or** strengths only **or** a comparative synopsis v a model performer.

For example, candidates may demonstrate acquired Knowledge and Understanding in respect of the:

Technical Qualities: Reference may be made to wide repertoire of skills eg *my dribbling, passing shooting etc is consistent and accurate*; this may be accompanied by clarification of success rate/quality of execution of preparation, action, recovery. For example, *like a model performer I execute my... with power* etc. Reference may also be made to the classification of skills demanded, for example, simple/complex etc.

Physical Qualities: Reference may be made to more than one aspect of fitness. To support acquired/applied Knowledge and Understanding the candidate must describe how the selected aspect of fitness affected performance. For example, my high levels of **Cardio Respiratory Endurance**, **Speed End** *helped me maintain pace and track my opponents continuously ... etc... my poor flexibility makes it difficult for me to... Unlike a model performer my lack of power meant that... etc.*

Personal Qualities: Reference may be made to inherent qualities, for example, **height** – *helped me to win rebounds consistently*, Other acceptable personal qualities such as being decisive/determined/confident/competitive etc, *put me at an advantage and intimidated my opponents... etc.*

Special Qualities: Reference may be made to the ability to create opportunity, disguise intent, make performance look more dynamic, apply flair, have the ability to choreograph routines/link complex skills... etc. For example, *these unique qualities helped me to fake my intent and so wrong foot my opponent/my routine was exciting to watch... or this helped me gain points etc.*

(c) *A good response should include some or most of the points as outlined below. The candidate's answer should include full detail with relevant examples to support specific strengths and weaknesses.*

Strengths and weaknesses

The responses will be wide ranging and relevant to the activity selected. Candidates may demonstrate acquired Knowledge and Understanding in respect of the specific role/team/solo responsibilities - strengths and weaknesses. Most likely a comparative analysis in relation to the identified technical, physical, personal and mental strengths and weaknesses will be evident in the candidates' answer.

Merit should be given according to depth and quality of description(s) and explanation(s) offered.

(d) *A good response should include some or most of the points as outlined below. The candidate's answer should include relevant detail to demonstrate acquired Knowledge and Understanding in relation to training considerations.*

Organisation of training

Within the response examples should include:

Knowledge of previously stated strengths and weaknesses. Setting of objectives/preparation for competitive event.

Decisions taken as a result of the performance weaknesses/ strengths reflective of appropriate training/development method(s) and or selected training regimes.
Training considerations offered should reflect and offer examples based on the: complexity of identified weaknesses, stage of learning, complexity of stacks etc.

Training considerations may include some or more of the following: training in/out of the activity/ conditioning approach, integrated training.

PREPARATION OF THE BODY

3. (a) *A good response should include some or most of the points as outlined below. The candidate may use different approaches to answer this question. They could select all three types of fitness or two types in detail and one type referring to the relevant aspects in detail.*

Physical skill related and mental types of fitness: You would expect the candidate to select the most appropriate type or more than one aspect within that type to show relevant Knowledge and Understanding to support the answer.

Physical fitness: Cardio Respiratory Endurance – speed – muscular endurance – flexibility – stamina – strength – aerobic/anaerobic endurance – speed endurance – power.

Skill related fitness: reaction time – agility – Knowledge and Understanding-ordination – balance – timing – movement anticipation.

Mental fitness: level of arousal – rehearsal – managing emotion – visualisation – motivation – determination – anxiety – managing stress – concentration.
All responses should make reference to how the types or aspect(s) chosen relate to **effective** performance in the activity.

Physical fitness: For example: *in football a high level of Cardio Respiratory Endurance and Speed Endurance allowed me to track and help my defence out… as well as support the attackers… throughout the whole game… also having good strength as a defender allowed me to jump and challenge for high balls and crosses… and win tackles against the opposition.*

Skill related fitness: For example: *in badminton having good agility will allow me quick movement… to reach the shuttle or change direction if necessary and return the shuttle to put my opponent under pressure – also… good timing will allow me to connect with the shuttle in the correct place and allow me to execute the shot correctly… hopefully leading to a successful outcome.*

Mental fitness: For example: *in basketball as the ball carrier by managing my emotions I was able to handle the pressure my opponent was putting on me when closely marking… I was able to make the correct decision and carry out the correct pass to my team mate successfully… also when I was taking a free throw, by managing my emotions and rehearsing my routine in my mind… I was able to execute the free throw successfully.*

(b) *A good response should include some or most of the points as outlined below. The candidate should show Knowledge and Understanding about the importance of gathering data.*

Gathering data: The responses will include the results arising from the information gathered and could include reference to specific fitness demands for the activity or perhaps the role within the activity. Reference should be made to the importance of analysing and the interpretation of results. This allows the candidate to establish pre training fitness levels and identify what they need to work on making specific reference to their strengths and weaknesses in terms of fitness. It provides a bench mark to work from. Specific and realistic targets can be set over a planned period of time. It also allows for the planning of a relevant training programme applying the principles of training. Knowledge of fitness levels before training allows comparison to be carried out with post training results. This allows monitoring to take place to see if the selected training programme has been successfully managed and carried out.

(c) *A good response should include some or most of the points as outlined below. The candidate should show both acquired and applied Knowledge and Understanding in relation to the training selected.*

Specific training types

A good response should have good description of the form of training selected.

In the activity(conditioning) – fartlek, short sprints and then continuous paced running with specific description of what they did. For example, *in athletics for 800 metre running I did fartlek training……did 8 laps …jogged the straights and ran the bends….done without stopping….then did 6 short 60 metre sprints …with a short 20 metre jog leading into each sprint … made demands similar to end of actual race*

Out with activity - could include circuit training/weight training with description of what they did/sets/reps/types of exercise For example, *to improve my Cardio Respiratory Endurance for my role as a midfielder in hockey … I trained out with activity… carried out some circuit training… doing high intensity work… work rest ratio 1:3… doing a series of exercises… step ups… burpees… continuous running… 3 sets of exercises… working on each from 45 secs*

Combination of both - continuous training in pool/weight training out of pool with appropriate description of each/involve some of the following methods fartlek/ continuous/conditioning/interval/circuit/weight training/relaxation/breathing/rehearsal

For example, *in swimming I trained using a combination of training within activity and out with activity… within I used interval training… working on developing both anaerobic and aerobic fitness… did warm up … then stroke improvement … main set 6x50 metre swim one minute recovery… sub set 6x50 …45 secs recovery… then warm down……out with pool did a weight training circuit… doing a series of exercises… …3 sets of exercises… also some work on stepping machines… rowing machines …to improve Cardio Respiratory Endurance .*

(d) *A good response should include some or most of the points as outlined below. The candidate should give an **explanation** as to why changes were made and then give examples to support the answer.*

Programme of work

The responses offered will be wide ranging and will depend on the candidate's choice of activity. For example, *training had reached a level where it was not demanding – achieved short term goals/boredom with training/apply overload apply principles of training/performance had stayed at same level/wanted to make progress in performance-motivation – variety increase workload.*

Examples should be given which relate to fitness being developed.

4. (a) *A good response should include some or most of the points as outlined below. The candidate should choose an appropriate method of collecting information and then **explain** why the method is appropriate.*

Skill related fitness
The aspects of fitness selected should be one of the following: reaction time/agility/co-ordination/balance/timing/movement anticipation.

The methods could include skill related observation schedules/standard fitness tests/game analysis/Knowledge of Results/video. The methods were appropriate because recognized national tests against norms identified/permanent record/provides evidence to compare progress/targets/ improvements/if video pause/rewind/aids motivation/provides qualitative/quantitative details of performance.

(b) *A good response should include some or most of the points as outlined below. The candidate should demonstrate Knowledge and Understanding with reference to the selected activity.*

Mental fitness: level of arousal – rehearsal – managing emotion – visualisation – motivation – determination – anxiety – managing stress – concentration. All responses should make reference to how the types or aspect(s) chosen relate to **effective** performance in the activity.

For example: *in basketball as the ball carrier by managing my emotions I was able to handle the pressure my opponent was putting on me when closely marking... I was able to make the correct decision and carry out the correct pass to my team mate successfully... also when I was taking a free throw, by managing my emotions and rehearsing my routine in my mind... I was able to execute the free throw successfully.*

(c) *A good response should include some or most of the points as outlined below. The candidate should include some detail of actual examples and must relate to physical fitness.*

Setting goals
A good response will highlight the importance of establishing short term goals to help reach longer term goals. Detailed examples should be offered to show understanding about performance gains as a result of setting realistic/attainable goals.
For example, *...inspires/motivates to do better... lets you see if training is working/needs to be progress... enables comparisons to be made... is a form of feedback... establishes achievement... can be used to judge performance against success criteria... etc.*

(d) *A good response should include some or most of the points as outlined below. The candidate should be able to show acquired knowledge.*

Planning and implementing
Reference to planning–based on nature and fitness demands of activity–role within activity/strengths and weaknesses/ time of season/may refer to S.M.A.R.T.E.R. Implementation/ principles of training/period of season/important that it is not just described but refers back to goals and physical fitness.

SKILLS AND TECHNIQUES

5. (a) *A good response should include some or most of the points as outlined below. The candidate should demonstrate acquired Knowledge and Understanding of Stages of Learning.*

Stages of Learning
A good response will include specific reference and detail appropriate with detailed explanations relevant to the stage of learning described.

Examples are often included to highlight their understanding in context; this may be generic or linked to a specific skill/technique.

For example, at the **cognitive stage** a performer will be reliant on a lot of instruction/feedback. The performer is learning about the sub routines of the skill/technique. Success rate/effectiveness is not refined etc.

At the **associative stage**, a performer will still be reliant on instruction/feedback but will be developing ability to self evaluate. The performer is more able to link the sub routines of the skill/technique; the execution of the skill is recognisable but the success rate/effectiveness is still not consistent or highly effective etc.

At the **automatic stage**, a performer will be less reliant on instruction/feedback with an ability to self evaluate and identify weaknesses. The performer is able to link the sub routines of the skill/technique; the execution of the skill is recognisable with control and consistency etc.

A link to other relevant factors may include; progressions possible from one stage to the next, model/skilled performer etc .

(b) *A good response should include some or most of the points as outlined below. The candidate should include full detail with relevant examples to support specific strengths and weaknesses.*

Practice considerations
A good response will include details relevant to the selection and appropriateness of the MOST relevant methods of practice/development/training available. Considerations of different methods will be evident in the process. Examples relevant to selected methods will be included highlighting the selections made.

For example, *at the cognitive stage, many shadow/repetition practices were incorporated to ensure... etc. At the associative stage some shadow/repetition practices progressing to combination drills... etc. At the automatic stage of learning more pressure/problem solving drills were used to advance and challenge learning and performance development.*

A link to other relevant factors may include; whole part, gradual build-up, mass/distributed, closed/open contexts etc.

(c) *A good response should include some or most of the points as outlined below. The candidate MUST include detailed description of the tools used.*

The monitoring process
The description of the method must be offered. Methods could include video, observation schedules/training diary/logbook. For example, *I used a training diary ... this allowed me to keep a note of my progress ... to see if my overall programme had improved.*

(d) *A good response should include some or most of the points as outlined below. The candidate MUST include detailed discussion about whole performance development.*

Whole performance development
A good response will highlight the impact of skill/technique development to WHOLE performance development. For example a more consistent application/less errors/more points won, a positive benefit including greater confidence etc.

The candidate may also include details referencing specific drills or parts of the programme that benefited their performance, for example, *I felt that the repetition drills such as... improved my ability to... etc.*

Similarly a comparative synopsis via a statistical % comparison before and after, or comparative to a model performer may also feature in the response.

Merit should be given to the feasibility/validity/justification for claims of improved performance.

6. (a) *A good response should include some or most of the points as outlined below. The candidate should include full detail with relevant examples to support Knowledge and Understanding.*

Features of a skilled performance
A good response will include reference to the range and qualities that are evident in a skilled/model performance. Reference should be made across the range of qualities displayed ie – technical, physical, skill and mental related.

A link to other relevant factors may include; wide repertoire of skills evident and executed at the correct time with consistency, fluency, ease of economy. Movements/application of skills seem effortless. Management of emotions are controlled. A degree of confidence. Few unforced errors. Makes appropriate decisions when under pressure etc.

(b) *A good response should include some or most of the points as outlined below. The candidate should include full detail with relevant examples to demonstrate acquired Knowledge and Understanding in the related areas of information processing and skill classification.*

Information Processing
Relevant description; this may be supported with use of a diagram. The description should include details appropriate to the skill/technique selected.

The four stages should appear in sequential order of:

- INPUT via stimuli/senses/instruction/demonstration or feedback offered.
- DECISION MAKING - action to be taken.
- OUTPUT - via taking appropriate action.
- EVALAUTION - what was the outcome of action taken; successful/unsuccessful, effective/ineffective.

Remediation process now occurs–repeat the action to develop/refine–regress to address weaknesses identified–progress to the next stage.

Skill classification
Relevant description of various types of skill. The description should include details appropriate to the skills selected inclusive of example. The classified skills likely to appear: Open/Closed. Discrete/Serial/Continuous. Simple/Complex.

Points highlighted:

- Open - dependent on different variables, externally paced eg a corner kick in football.
- Closed - Internally paced, performer is almost in total control, eg a drive in golf.
- Discrete - clear beginning and end, requiring fine motor skills.
- Serial - a combination of discrete skills which performed in sequence produces a unique skill such as lay-up in Basketball
- Continuous - no clear pattern of beginning or end such as swimming
- Simple - requiring few sub routines, no element of danger eg forward roll in gymnastics
- Complex - many sub routines, element of danger eg front somersault in gymnastics.

(c) *A good response should include some or most of the points as outlined below. The candidate MUST include detailed description about the tools used. Simply naming the method is not sufficient.*

Appropriate methods of data collection
Description of the method(s) used must be offered; a diagram will often feature to support answer. The appropriateness of the methods described should enable either qualitative or quantative details of performance progress. A range of relevant methods will be selected from: movement/mechanical or consideration of quality.

Explanations offered about appropriateness may include, it provides evidence to compare progress/targets/improvements. It is a permanent record, can be used time and time again, aids motivation, and ensures further challenge and progress, information can be gathered at the beginning/middle and end etc. If video is used reference will be made to pause/rewind facility etc.

(d) *A good response should include some or most of the points as outlined below.*

Programme of work
The responses offered will be wide ranging and will depend on the candidate's choice of skill/technique identified for development.

Programme references may include details of weeks 1& 2, weeks 3& 4, weeks 5& 6, etc. or *I used a gradual build up/whole part whole approach to my development programme.* In this respect the notion of reliability/validity should be apparent and justified etc.

The content and structure given must be justified with progressions exemplified to demonstrate sound Knowledge and Understanding. For example, *As I was at the cognitive stage I used many shadow/repetition practices to ensure… etc . At the associative stage I used some shadow/repetition practices progressing to combination drills… etc . At the automatic stage of learning I knew to use more pressure/problem solving drills as these would challenge me more… etc. I found the … skill very difficult so decided to use gradual build up as this would… etc. In weeks 1 & 2, I concentrated more on simple drills… in weeks 3-4, I progressed to more complex drills such as… etc. This built my confidence as I reached my target of… etc.*

A link to other relevant factors may include; whole part, gradual build up, mass/distributed, closed/open contexts, repetitions, target setting, model performers etc.

Importantly, the response must include reference to reviewing the programme of work. Details should include some of the following: it provides evidence to compare progress/targets/improvements, aids motivation, ensures further challenge and progress, highlights whether programme was successful and appropriate for skill development and stage of learning.

STRUCTURES, STRATEGIES AND COMPOSITIONS

7. (a) *A good response should include some or most of the points as outlined below. The candidate should show acquired Knowledge and Understanding as to why it is important to gather information on selected Structures, Strategies and Compositions.*

Information gathering
Find out the strengths and weaknesses of your team/your role in team/of opposition/find out if your Structures, Strategies and Compositions is effective or requires change/to suit particular needs/to inform decisions about the future/able to plan a programme of practice to implement Structures, Strategies and Compositions more effectively.

Examples should be given of the strengths and weaknesses identified.

(b) *A good response should include some or most of the points as outlined below. The candidate is required to **describe** how they addressed weaknesses and **explain** the actions. They are required to show applied Knowledge and Understanding.*

Programme of work

They will describe a programme of work taking cognisance of weaknesses described previously: a range of programmes may be offered including practising parts in isolation; unopposed/opposed practices/games. The content and structure must be justified with possible progressions within programme to explain the actions.

Candidates may also change or adopt the Structures, Strategies and Compositions either as individuals or as a team as a short term measure.

(c) *A good response should include some or most of the points as outlined below. The candidate is expected to show acquired Knowledge and Understanding as to why monitoring is important.*

Monitoring

It provides evidence to compare progress/targets/ improvements; aids motivation; gives evidence on whether programme of work carried out has been effective; checking whether training methods were appropriate; ensures progress and further development; gives feedback on your performance; training at correct intensity; if improvements were made in areas/weaknesses you targeted; making sure you are not overworking; analyse your training on an ongoing basis; information to plan adjustments to your training.

(d) *A good response should include some or most of the points as outlined below. The candidate is expected to show applied knowledge in two selected principles/fundamentals selected.*

Structures, Strategies and Composition fundamentals and principles

Speed in attack: for example the candidate may (in fast break in basketball) show importance of getting ahead of the ball and the opposition to score an easy lay-up/unopposed shot or create overload. *In basketball I wanted to play a fast tempo game… attack quickly… so I made sure that on each opportunity we tried to play a fast break… to catch the defence out… score a quick basket … create an overload situation… before the defence was organised properly.*

Width depth mobility: in any activity game area a team should successfully cover the width as well as length (depth) of area/also team should adapt and respond to change of either team Structures, Strategies and Composition or tactics of opposition.
Importance of creativity: in gymnastics the types of actions/movements in a particular sequence/linking movements together/allow sequence to flow/score more marks.

Using repetition, variation and contrast: in dance, similar to above in gymnastics, but using different levels/movements for variation/contrast/repeating movements within dance.

In all, the Knowledge and Understanding is to explain the importance when applying the selected Structures, Strategies and Compositions.

8. (a) *A good response should include some or most of the points as outlined below. The candidate should include detailed description and acquired knowledge of the Structure, Strategy or Compositions selected.*

Structures, Strategies and Composition

The candidate must describe in detail the Structures, Strategies or Compositions. Some will also make reference possibly to the role they played as well.

These will include:

- fast break/zones/1-3-1/horse shoe offence in basketball/man/man defence
- Football – 4-2-4/4-3-3/3-5-2
- Badminton – front-back-side-side
- Gymnastics particular sequence-routine
- Volleyball – rotation
- Hockey – penalty corner
- Dance – a particular dance or routine used

(b) *A good response should include some or most of the points as outlined below. The candidate should show applied Knowledge and Understanding and discuss the problems that they faced. Their answer should show detailed **discussion** on some or more of the following points.*

Structures, Strategies and Composition problems

Problems will probably be described with outcome of problem and then discussed. Examples may refer to the role in Structures, Strategies and Composition; the skills/weaknesses of individuals/team when applying Structures, Strategies and Composition; link to the Structures, Strategies and Composition being applied by opposition; pressures of performing to spectators; time restrictions applied; strengths and weaknesses of opposition.

(c) *A good response should include some or most of the points as outlined below. The candidate should show Knowledge and Understanding of how the problems mentioned previously were addressed. This will require the candidate to be able to use decision making and problem solving. The candidate should show detailed **discussion**.*

Decision making and problem solving

Cognisance of problems mentioned. Reference will be made to possible changes to Structures, Strategies and Composition either as individuals or as part of a team; a range of development programmes will be evident; the structure should be justified as well as the content; the Structures, Strategies and Composition may be adapted to cope with problem.

(d) *A good response should include some or most of the points as outlined below. The candidate should **explain** how they evaluated improvements to Structures, Strategies and Composition.*

Evaluation

Methods selected to gather information on improvements: video-game analysis; observation schedules; Knowledge of Results; criteria check lists; statistics; personal reflection; feedback internal/external; comparison to previous information gathered.

HIGHER PHYSICAL EDUCATION 2008

In the Higher Physical Education examination candidates will answer from the perspective of their experiences in a wide variety of activities. An activity specific answer section would result in an enormous document which would be extremely cumbersome and time-consuming to use and which could never realistically cover all possibilities.

In relation to **all** questions it should be noted that the relevance of the content in the candidates' responses will depend on:

- the activity selected
- the performance focus
- the training/development programme/programme of work selected
- the practical experiences of their course as the contexts for answers.

PERFORMANCE APPRECIATION

1. (a) *A good response should include some or most of the points as outlined below. To demonstrate acquired Knowledge and Understanding the candidate's response should include descriptive detail about their* **personal** *performance in relation to two specific qualities.*

    Qualities: In relation to **any** of the qualities selected a detailed personal description should be offered. In this respect the candidate may elect to answer from the viewpoint of having a positive or negative effect on performance. Similarly the description could be offered *via* a synopsis of strengths and weaknesses **or** strengths only **or** a comparative synopsis v a model performer.

    For example, candidates may demonstrate acquired Knowledge and Understanding in respect of the:

    Technical Qualities: Reference may be made to wide repertoire of skills eg *my dribbling, passing shooting etc is consistent and accurate*; this may be accompanied by clarification of success rate/quality of execution of preparation, action, recovery. For example, *like a model performer I execute my… with power* etc.

    Physical Qualities: Reference may be made to more than one aspect of fitness. To support acquired/applied Knowledge and Understanding the candidate must describe how the selected aspect of fitness affected performance. For example, my high levels of **Cardio Respiratory Endurance**, **Speed End** *helped me maintain pace and track my opponents continuously … etc… my poor flexibility makes it difficult for me to… Unlike a model performer my lack of power meant that…* etc.

    Personal Qualities: Reference may be made to inherent qualities, for example, **height** – *helped me to win rebounds consistently*. Other acceptable personal qualities could include being decisive/determined/confident/competitive etc, *put me at an advantage and intimidated my opponents…* etc.

    Special Qualities: Reference may be made to the ability to create opportunity, disguise intent, make performance look more dynamic, apply flair, have the ability to choreograph routines/link complex skills… etc. For example, *these unique qualities helped me to fake my intent and so wrong foot my opponent/my routine was exciting to watch… or this helped me gain points etc.*

    (b) *A good response should include some or most of the points as outlined below. The candidate's response should include full details about how reliable information was gathered.*

    Gathering data: Description of the method(s) used may be offered; a diagram will often feature to support answer. In context of the answer candidates should reference the *'process'* ie how the data was collected. A narrative account of **what** was done and **why** should be obvious; thus demonstrating logical thinking. Evidence of critical thinking should be apparent in the selection/detail of the method(s) selected as this should enable the candidate to gather either/or both qualitative/quantitative details of performance strengths and weaknesses in whole performance; in this respect the notion of reliability/validity should be apparent.

    NOTE *'face validity'* of candidates' choice should be accepted in this instance. For example, *whole* performance skills/fitness/qualities may be gathered via reliable methods such as video, performance profiles, scattergrams, match analysis sheet, fitness tests, etc.

    Most likely, the process offered in the responses will examine *Initial data* collection then *Focussed* to value the identification of Strengths and Weaknesses.

    (c) *A good response should include some or most of the points as outlined below. The candidate should demonstrate a level of critical thinking when considering the benefits of using models of performance.*

    ### The use of model performance
    A good response will include reference to the impact on learning and/or developing a specific part of their performance. Most likely this will pertain to skill learning/development. For example, using a model performer can advantage performance or developmental process in a number of ways.

    ### Model performers
    Explanations offered about the importance/benefits/ advantages of considering model performers may include the opportunity for less experienced performers to:

    - observe quality/effortless performance and/or application of skills
    - compare before/after development
    - monitor progress/targets
    - increase motivation
    - provides challenge (s)
    - provide meaningful feedback
    - mirror training/practices
    - copy the execution of skill/technique
    - inspire design ideas
    - be given accurate feeds/placement
    - make quicker progress/can make progress quicker
    - prevent bad habits from forming etc.

    (d) *A good response should include some or most of the points as outlined below. The candidate's response should include detailed discussion to demonstrate thorough Knowledge and Understanding about the importance of goal setting. In this context both acquired and applied knowledge is examined.*

    Goal setting: A good response will highlight the need to consider short-term goals to enable achievement of long-term goal status.
    A reference to planning is crucial as there is a need to think about **both** immediate and long-term achievements. Some candidates may also refer to mid-term goals others may link goal setting to training goals demonstrating related Knowledge and Understanding of phases of training; pre/mid/competitive or micro, meso, macro.
    Regardless of the tact taken, the candidate should demonstrate detailed Knowledge and Understanding by showing critical thinking, for example:

considering my short term goals eg to maintain general fitness, refinement of technical/mental/special abilities etc, this enabled me to work towards my longer-term goals such as developing more specific aspects of fitness/skills etc, this in turn for example improves tactical plans and enables more practiced alternatives to be applied or adapted when in competitive situations, etc.

The candidate should demonstrate critical thinking when exemplifying specific examples of personal goals set. The examples must be relevant and justified.

A link to other important factors may feature, such as increases motivation/determination, highlights where weaknesses require further improvement or where strengths are maintained, ensures pacing/progression of training/practice, ensures working towards a common aim/enables before and after comparisons to be made/helps reflect success and establishes future goals, etc.

2. (a) *A good response should include some or most of the points as outlined below. The candidate's response should include full detail with relevant examples to demonstrate acquired Knowledge and Understanding. It is perfectly acceptable that the candidate may offer from an individual/team perspective.*

   Mental factors: A good response will include detailed Knowledge and Understanding about the effects of cognitive and/or somatic anxiety, state of arousal/managing emotions/dealing with stress. Other points raised may include lack of concentration, self-belief or confidence etc.

   Reference may be made to the potential *effects* of positive and negative mental factors on performance and/or the internal/intrinsic, external/extrinsic effects. For example, *a positive influence* will impact upon performance by increasing state of mind/state of arousal and so enable the performer to produce sound levels of effectiveness/perform at maximum potential level/handle the pressure and remain calm/make appropriate decisions and enable appropriate actions in response to the immediate situation. There may be heightened awareness/confidence/early preparedness/few unforced errors/sustained performance standards and production of consistent application of skills to deal with the performance context. Reference may also be made to Knowledge of Performance/Knowledge of Results or external factors such as crowd, level of competition and rewards.

   Conversely – *a negative influence* will impact performance producing an ineffective/erratic and unconfident performance, apprehension before; cognitive anxiety, and during performance, nerves get the better; somatic anxiety – physiological response, and so more unforced errors/fouls/made, severe lapse of concentration which may cause poor decision making or an inability to stick to role related duties associated with application of structure/strategy, etc.

   (b) *A good response should include some or most of the points as outlined below. The candidate should reference how the selected mental factor affected performance in a negative way. In this context both acquired and applied knowledge is examined as the candidate is also required to highlight which method(s) helped them to manage the situation.*

   Mental factors: The candidate should highlight the specific aspect of mental fitness, such as dealing with cognitive/somatic anxiety, managing emotions, level of arousal – over or under arousal. The selected factor must be relevant and the effect on performance justified. For example, *cognitive anxiety affected my self confidence, motivation/concentration prior to me starting my game…The very thought of going on court made me panic.., I could not overcome my fear and so…. etc.*

   Accompanying the examples offered there should be sufficient depth and quality of explanation to exhibit applied Knowledge and Understanding in context. For example, *As part of my warm up I used deep breathing, self talk, mental rehearsal, visualisation to keep me calm etc.*

   Crucially the candidate must justify why the selected method(s) were appropriate. For example, *self talk was appropriate as it is quick to use… Key/trigger words give me a boost; concentration is increased… etc… visualisation helps me go over in my mind how to execute the shot… I can complete this instantly and so groove my focus and imagine the shot going in, etc.*

   (c) *A good response should include some or most of the points as outlined below. The candidate's response should include full detail with relevant examples to demonstrate applied Knowledge and Understanding from the programme of work used.*

   Weakness: As the structure of the question is open-ended, the responses offered will be wide ranging. The candidate should however cite the weakness in relation to either a technical, physical, personal and mental factors relevant to their performance. For example, the complexity of identified skill, stage of learning, complexity of task, level of fitness; in this respect the notion of validity should be apparent and justified.

   Merit should be given according to depth/quality/relevance of improvement programme offered. Crucially the link to how this programme was planned and managed must be made. For example, *'the process'* planning considerations may include some or more of the following:
   * whether to train in/out of the activity
   * the merits of using a conditioning approach or to integrate training

   Management considerations may include, for example:
   * duration of programme
   * applying principles of practice/training as appropriate
   * feedback/monitoring etc

   Most likely the candidate will give specific examples, for example:
   * *In weeks 1-2 I used …, in weeks 3-4 …*
   * *I then introduced … as this helped to ….*
   * *Finally in weeks 5-6, I knew to … etc.*

   (d) *A good response should include some or most of the points as outlined below. The candidate's response should include full detail to support applied Knowledge and Understanding from the review process.*

   The review process: A good response will include specific points about the importance/purpose of the 'process', for example:
   * it may provide qualitative or quantitative details of whether the programme is effective/working
   * it substantiates specific fitness/skill progress
   * it makes sure that overload/progressions can be applied as appropriate, etc.

   Explanations offered about the effectiveness may include:
   * it provides evidence to compare progress/targets/improvements
   * enables changes/adaptations to be made during my programme to ensure further challenge and progress
   * it promotes motivation and challenge.

PREPARATION OF THE BODY

3. (a) *A good response should include some or most of the points as outlined below. The candidate must demonstrate acquired Knowledge and Understanding in the description of how each type of fitness contributes to effective performance within the selected activity.*

Physical, skill related and mental types of fitness: You would expect the candidate to select the most appropriate type or more than one aspect within that type to show relevant Knowledge and Understanding to support the answer.

Physical fitness: Cardio Respiratory Endurance – speed – muscular endurance – flexibility – stamina – strength – aerobic/anaerobic endurance – speed endurance – power.

Skill related fitness: reaction time – agility – co-ordination – balance – timing – movement anticipation.

Mental fitness: level of arousal – rehearsal – managing emotion – visualisation – motivation – determination – anxiety – managing stress – concentration.
All responses should make reference to how the type (s) or aspect(s) chosen relate to **effective** performance in the activity.

Physical fitness: For example: *in football a high level of Cardio Respiratory Endurance and speed endurance allowed me to track and help my defence out... as well as support the attackers... throughout the whole game... also having good strength as a defender allowed me to jump and challenge for high balls and crosses... and win tackles against the opposition.*

Skill related fitness: For example: *in badminton having good agility will allow me quick movement... to reach the shuttle or change direction if necessary and return the shuttle to put my opponent under pressure – also... good timing will allow me to connect with the shuttle in the correct place and allow me to execute the shot correctly... hopefully leading to a successful outcome.*

Mental fitness: For example: *in basketball as the ball carrier by managing my emotions I was able to handle the pressure my opponent was putting on me when closely marking... I was able to make the correct decision and carry out the correct pass to my team mate successfully... when I was also taking a free throw by managing my emotions and rehearsing my routine in my mind... I was able to execute the free throw successfully.*

(b) *A good response should include some or most of the points as outlined below. The candidate must select an appropriate aspect and give a description and explanation as to how they gathered information on it **within** the activity.*

Gathering data– The description of the method could be within the activity. A diagram may feature in the answer, for example, a time related observation schedule within football, showing information relevant to the particular aspect selected which was speed end/Cardio Respiratory Endurance. In the answer the candidate should make reference to the process used to gather the information. A narrative account of what was done and **why** should be obvious showing logical thinking. Methods could include video/performance profiles/checklists/scattergrams/ Preparation, Action, Recovery/stroke counts/breath counts/pulse counts/feedback - reliability and validity of method should be apparent. Standard fitness tests would not be appropriate as they would normally be carried out with the activity.

(c) *A good response should include some or most of the points as outlined below. The candidate must demonstrate both acquired and applied Knowledge and Understanding in relation to each phase of training.*

Phases of training: Answers are expected to have a description of what they did in each phase and to explain what each particular stage means and to give specific examples

of training covered. For example in the **preparation phase (preseason)** candidates will refer to general fitness work being developed to build up endurance whereas in the **competition phase (during the season)** they may be working on specific aspects of fitness/skills for competition. Fine tuning of skills and working on specific strategies would be apparent in this phase compared to the preseason where more general working on skills would happen.
In the **transition phase (off season)** you would expect responses to refer to the body recovering after competition and maintaining a general/reasonable level of fitness maybe by doing some alternative activities like swimming or cycling.

Examples in:
Preparation (preseason) could include general running/circuit training/particular drills
Competition (during the season) could include a strength/fitness training program to improve a particular part of fitness which is vital in game or working on a particular penalty corner drill for hockey
Transition (off season) could include swimming, cycling as an alternative activity and a basic circuit to keep your fitness ticking over.

Reasons for particular differences given between each stage should show relevant Knowledge and Understanding. For example, the **preparation phase (preseason)** is about building up fitness in a general way whereas the **competition phase (during the season)** is about reaching a particular level and then looking at improving specific fitness.

(d) *A good response should include some or most of the points as outlined below. The candidate must select an appropriate method of training and describe what they did. They must also provide an explanation as to why it was appropriate.*

Methods of training
The candidates responses will be wide ranging and depend on the choice of activity and the type or aspect of fitness selected. Various methods of training could be chosen and some candidates may choose one session or a block of time to describe what they did. Knowledge and Understanding should be shown with regards training selected and as to the appropriateness. Training could be within activity/outwith/ combination and involve some of the following methods – fartlek/continuous/conditioning/interval/circuit/weight training/relaxation/breathing/rehearsal.

For example:
I used interval training for swimming... warm up of 8 lengths multi stroke... then some stroke improvement... then main set... 6 × 50 metre swim with a minute rest between each set... then sub set...
6 × 50... 45 second recovery. This was appropriate because it enables high intensity work combined with rest to allow me to train for a longer period of time and thus gaining greater benefits from training.

Appropriateness can involve activity specific movements to develop both skill and fitness demands/can simulate the pressure demands/can be fun and motivational/easy to carry out/little or no equipment necessary/can develop both general and specific muscles/variety.

4. (a) *A good response should include some or most of the points as outlined below. The candidate must describe in detail a situation where fitness was a strength and a weakness in their performance.*

Strengths and weaknesses
Candidates will most likely describe a situation using a type or types of fitness to answer the question. Some may use

the same activity or answer using two different activities. Relevant Knowledge and Understanding should be apparent in the response in relation to activity and the situation. The effect on performance will be referred to as a result of the strength and weakness identified.

For example, strength:
when playing basketball… in the last seconds… the match was even …. an opponent shot…missed… as a centre physical fitness was a strength… it helped me block out my opponent… allowing me to get the rebound for my team and ….deliver an outlet pass to start a fast break… which we scored from …to win the game.

For example, weakness:
my Cardio Respiratory Endurance was a problem in football …late in the game…. I lost the ball when attacking the person … marking me in midfield…. I did not have the stamina to chase back… and dispossess him … he went on to score a goal.

(b) *A good response should include some or most of the points as outlined below. The candidate must demonstrate acquired knowledge in their description of a method of training appropriate to a strength or weakness identified.*

Methods of training

The candidates responses will be wide ranging and depend on the choice of activity and the type or aspect of fitness selected. It must also be relevant to the strength or weakness identified in part (a) of the question. Various methods of training could be chosen and some candidates may choose one session or a block of time to describe what they did. Knowledge and Understanding should be shown with regards method of training selected and as to the appropriateness. Training could be withinactivity/outwith/ combination and involve some of the following methods – fartlek/continuous/ conditioning/interval/circuit/weight training/relaxation/ breathing/rehearsal.

For example, *for my weakness of cardio respiratory endurance I decided to do conditioning ……I trained within activity … carried out some circuit training… doing high intensity work… work rest ratio 1:3… doing a series of exercises… working on fitness… also practicing particular skills I use within a game…*

(c) *A good response should include some or most of the points as outlined below. The candidate must demonstrate both acquired and applied Knowledge and Understanding with regards principles of training when designing and completing training programme.*

Principles of training

The answer must refer to the principles of training. Most of the following principles should be referred to: specificity to activity/person/performance – progressive overload – frequency – intensity – duration – adaptation – rest/recovery/over training/reversibility.
You will probably have detail or description of how they were applied to programme and also explanation and justification why they were considered.

For example:
I made sure the training was specific to the weakness identified… also demands of activity… I trained 3 times per week with rest every other… allowed body to recover… applied overload after week 3… increased number of sets… training became harder and body adapted to new load… as I was getting fitter… variety within programme… prevent boredom and keep motivation high.

(d) *A good response should include some or most of the points as outlined below. The candidate must demonstrate relevant Knowledge and Understanding and show critical thinking about the importance of evaluating their training programme.*

The evaluating process

A good response will show knowledge about the purpose and importance of the process. It may provide qualitative or quantitative details of whether the training is effective/working – it can substantiate the specific fitness progress – explanations may include/provide evidence to compare progress/targets/ improvements – enables changes to be made – ensure future targets – further challenges – promotes motivation – whether training method was appropriate – deciding if training was at correct intensity.

SKILLS AND TECHNIQUES

5. (a) *A good response should include some or most of the points as outlined below. The candidate's response should demonstrate acquired Knowledge and Understanding about related factors that will influence learning and or performance.*

Motivation/Concentration/Feedback

Two out of three influential factors **must** be selected. In this respect the candidate may give a detailed synopsis of how **each** factor selected impacted upon their *learning* and or their *application* of skill/technique. Merit should be given according to depth/quality/relevance of explanations offered.

NOTE – it is likely that similar points may be referenced/ exemplified in relation to discrete factor.

Motivation: A good response will include details of being internally (intrinsic)/externally (extrinsic) motivated to learn/achieve success. Being motivated enables the performer to be self driven to listen to instruction and act on it, it helps the performer to be self determined/give of their best/come from behind/respond to immediate problems/competitive challenges/not worry if mistakes are made and re-channel focus.

Concentration: A good response will include details of the need to concentrate/focus on instruction/demonstration offered to ensure effective execution/application of skill or technique, promotes progression/adaptation of skill or technique, ensures bad habits are not formed/eradicated, enables the performer to perform their role and apply their skills appropriately, promotes the ability to read play/make effective decisions/adapt to the immediate situation etc. In the context of games, concentration enables the performer to stick to role related duties/application of structure/strategy/game plan etc.

Feedback: A good response will include details of receiving internal (kinaesthetic) feedback to progress/refine skill or technique **or** receiving/giving external feedback visual/ verbal/written/vestibular), to progress/refine skill or technique of self or that of others.

Feedback should be positive/immediate to promote confidence/success.

(b) *A good response should include some or most of the points as outlined below. The candidate should include a description of a relevant programme of work to develop an identified skill or technique. The programme offered should be justified.*

Programme of work

The responses offered will be wide ranging and will depend on the candidate's choice of activity and skill/technique identified for development. The programme followed should be detailed with reference made to some of the following considerations: Stages of Learning, skill complexity/skill classification. The candidate may offer from a 'one session' or '6-8 week' perspective, in this respect the notion of reliability/validity should be apparent and justified

For example:
As I was at the cognitive stage – I used many shadow/repetition practices to ensure… etc. At the automatic stage of learning I knew to use more pressure/problem solving drills as these would challenge me more…etc I found the .. skill very difficult so decided to use gradual build up as this would … etc. .. In weeks 1&2, I concentrated more on simple drills… in weeks 3-4, I progressed to more complex drills such as …. etc this built my confidence as I reached my target of… etc

A link to other relevant factors may include:
whole part, gradual build up, mass/distributed, closed/open contexts, repetitions, target setting, model performers etc.

(c) *A good response should include some or most of the points as outlined below. The candidate's response should demonstrate sound Knowledge and Understanding about the principles of effective practice with exemplification of HOW these were applied. In this context both acquired and applied knowledge is examined.*

Principles of effective practice
Often the acronym S.M.A.R.T.E.R. features in the candidate's answer. A good response will include a systematic discussion of each of the principles inclusive of exemplification of how these principles were applied to the programme described in part b). For example, practice should be specific, measurable, attainable, realistic, time related, exciting and regular… *as my programme was specific it helped me to achieve success… I could target the specific part of my technique that needed most improvement. I knew to set targets and raise them once… this ensured my practice was motivating* etc.

Other relevant knowledge will reference to factors such as practice needs to show progression to ensure targets were reached/enabled refinement/remediation/regression as required, increased motivation, improved confidence, consideration of work rest ratio etc.

(d) *A good response should include some or most of the points as outlined below. The candidate's response should demonstrate detailed discussion about whole performance development.*

Whole performance development
A good response will highlight the impact of skill/technique development to WHOLE performance development. For example a more consistent application/less errors/more points won, a positive benefit including greater confidence etc.

The candidate may also include details referencing specific drills or parts of the programme that benefited their performance, for example, *I felt that the repetition drills such as… improved my ability to… etc.*
Similarly a comparative synopsis via a statistical % comparison before and after, or comparative to a model performer may also feature in the response.

Merit should be given to the feasibility/validity/justification for claims of improved performance.

6. (a) *A good response should include some or most of the points as outlined below. The candidate's response should include full detail with relevant examples to demonstrate acquired Knowledge and Understanding.*

Data methods
The method selected will be wide ranging. A good response will include detail about the process. In a systematic way the

candidate should exhibit sound level of critical thinking by highlighting **what** was done. For example-First – *whole/initial performance*, analysis via valid methods such as: video/Match Analysis Sheet/Observation sheets/ performance profiles/questionnaires etc THEN *specific/focussed* analysis via valid methods such as video/Match Analysis Sheet/Observation sheets; inclusive of specific success criteria/performance profiles/questionnaires etc.

NOTE – some data tools used may feature in more than one collection type; this is acceptable. Also diagrams of methods used often feature to support depth of answer.

Acceptable examples of methods of gathering data may include:

Movement Analysis: Video, Observation Checklist, Match Analysis Sheet/scattergram/ questionnaires, PAR sheets, Comparison to model performers etc

Mechanical Analysis: Video, Observation Checklist, questionnaires, PAR sheets of force, levers, propulsion etc

Consideration of Quality: reflecting on movement skill execution being controlled/fluent, or fast/slow etc via video, Observation Checklist, questionnaires, PAR sheets, Comparison to model performers etc reflecting on controlled/fluent, or fast/slow

NOTE in the candidate's description of the method(s) selected the relevance of criteria **must** be justified. For example if the candidate names a 'mechanical analysis sheet' but proceeds to highlight the details pertaining to a movement analysis method such as Match Analysis Sheet then this exhibits poor acquired Knowledge and Understanding.

(b) *A good response should include some or most of the points as outlined below. The candidate's response should demonstrate critical thinking in the evaluation of highlighted strengths and weaknesses to whole performance.*

Analysis of Strengths and Weaknesses
The quality of the analysis offered by the candidate may reflect both Strengths and Weaknesses or Weaknesses only *or* may reflect the comparisons to that of a model performer *or* may reflect a statistical % of success rate when performing.

Irrespective of the tack taken, the candidate must demonstrate critical thinking by offering a degree of authenticity in their analysis, crucially this must be substantiated when referenced to the methods used in part a).

Importantly the candidate must emphasise how their **whole** performance was affected. For example, *my inaccurate shooting meant that I… this in turn affected my confidence and execution of other skills… looking at my scattergram I had a high % of my shots landing… a poor preparation phase in my smash meant that I was not behind the shuttle when hitting it this caused me to lose power …etc. A link to other factors such as reduced confidence, affected other parts of game/performance may be evident.*

(c) *A good response should include some or most of the points as outlined below. The candidate's response should demonstrate Knowledge and Understanding about the design of the programme followed. In this context both acquired and applied knowledge is examined.*

Programme of work
The responses offered will be wide ranging and will depend on the candidate's choice of skill/technique identified for development in part b).

The response must include details of the considerations/ critical debate about the selection and appropriateness of the methods of practice/development programme followed. In this respect the candidate should be convincing in their argument about **why** one method was selected in preference to another- ie the *'process'* should be obvious and justified. The programme followed should be described with reference made to some of the following considerations: Stage of Learning, Skill complexity/Skill classification, model performer, Feedback, Goal Setting etc. Programme references may include details of weeks 1 & 2, weeks 3 & 4, weeks 5 & 6 etc *or* I used a gradual build up/WPW approach to my development programme etc.

The content and structure given **must** be justified with progressions exemplified to demonstrate Knowledge and Understanding.

For example, at the cognitive stage:
many shadow/repetition practices were incorporated to ensure … etc. At the associative stage some shadow/repetition practices progressing to combination drills, etc. At the automatic stage of learning more pressure/problem solving drills were used to advance and challenge learning and performance development…. Using a gradual build up to improve my handspring was appropriate as it gave me confidence at each specific stage and so I… etc.

(d) *A good response should include some or most of the points as outlined below.*

The importance of monitoring and reviewing
A good response will highlight the differences/benefits of the purpose of monitoring = ongoing process. Such as reference to appropriate data methods to facilitate comparison of improvements, achieving targets set, gaining and acting on feedback, aids motivation, ensures further challenge and progress.

Importantly, the response must include reference to reviewing performance = summative progress. The structure of the question may enable the candidate to offer a 'holistic' overview – this is deemed acceptable.

Many candidates will repeat or include some of the previously mentioned comments. However reference to the evaluation of the **whole** process ie the impact of the training/development programme/programme of work should be highlighted. Judgements on the success/effectiveness of the programme/ used **plus** judgements on the success/effectiveness to whole performance must be clearly defined.

STRUCTURES, STRATEGIES AND COMPOSITIONS

7. (a) *A good response should include some or most of the points as outlined below. The candidate must demonstrate acquired Knowledge and Understanding regarding Structure, Strategy or Composition selected and be able to describe the strengths they had when applying it.*

Structures, Strategies and Composition
The candidate must describe the Structure, Strategy or Composition. Some will also make reference possibly to the role they played as well.

These will include:

- fast break/zones/1-3-1/horse shoe offence in basketball/man/man defence
- Football-4-2-4/4-3-3/3-5-2
- Badminton front-back-side-side
- Gymnastics particular sequence-routine
- Volleyball-rotation
- Hockey penalty corner-

The answers must also include their strengths. Some candidates may answer by referring to the strengths as a team or as strengths as an individual.
For example, *in tennis I used a serve volley strategy … I would serve fast and hard to opponent … follow my serve … get into net and position quickly … use a volley to win point … from opponents return*
My strengths were I had a consistent and fast first serve … high percentage of being in … quick to get to net … good forehand volley technique … made winners from first volley.

(b) *A good response should include some or most of the points as outlined below. The candidate must demonstrate applied Knowledge and Understanding of how they planned to make best use of strengths when performing. They must show critical thinking.*

Planning
The answers may vary according to the Structure, Strategy or Composition selected. The following factors may be apparent in answers: to use particular players with particular roles; strengths of these players; type of opposition; attack/defence being applied by my team or opposition; time restrictions in game; after a particular time or situation in activity; ground/weather conditions; prior or previous knowledge of opponent(s)-previous results.

For example, *Having played against my opponent previously … I knew his backhand was weak … so I made sure I served to that side … this led to a poor return … also I had forced my opponent out wide in service area … led often to me volleying an outright winner.*

(c) *A good response should include some or most of the points as outlined below. The candidate must be able to describe the weakness(es) they had when applying Structures, Strategies and Compositions and demonstrate detailed discussion on the effect on their performance.*

Weaknesses effect on performance
The answers must include their weakness(es).
Some candidates may answer by referring to the weakness(es) as a team or as an individual. They must show critical thinking by offering a degree of authenticity in their analysis and should make reference as to how their whole performance was affected.

For example:
My backhand volley was poor … made most errors from this technique … usually went into net or out of court … lost many points … poor second serve … often too short … opponents exploit this leading to lost points … exploitation by opponent … passed on many occasions. Also a link to other factors such as reduced confidence, lack of fitness etc may be evident in the answers.

(d) *A good response should include some or most of the points as outlined below. The candidate must demonstrate relevant critical thinking and decision making to explain how the effect of the weakness(es) were reduced.*

Weaknesses addressed
The responses offered will be wide ranging and will depend on the choice of Structures, Strategies and Compositions selected and the weakness(es) identified. The responses could be a description of the programme of work followed but this must be relevant to weakness mentioned. For example: *for my backhand volley I carried out a skill development programme… partner threw me a ball… play a backhand volley… gradually increased speed and distance… added more pressure… eventually to full speed …then aim for targets on court… two feeders drive me the ball from back of court …alternate backhand /forehand volley… serve to partner*

and get them to return to backhand side to play volley

Various methods of training/practice may be described – reference may be made to possible changes to Structures, Strategies and Composition either as individuals or as part of a team… a range of development programmes will be evident, the structure should be evident as well as the content, the Structures, Strategies and Composition may be changed or adapted to overcome weakness(es)… substitute player. Responses must show critical thinking and relevant decision making and should reduce the effect of weakness(es) on performance.

8. (a) *A good response should include some or most of the points as outlined below. The candidate must demonstrate applied Knowledge and Understanding about the factors considered when selecting a Structures, Strategies and Composition.*

The responses will be wide ranging and will depend on the choice of Structures, Strategies and Composition selected. Responses will include some of the following: strengths and weaknesses of your own team; strengths and weaknesses of the opposition; particular strengths of individual players within the Structures, Strategies and Composition; experience of players in team or opposition; previous results; how long you can apply the Structures, Strategies and Composition; score in the game; time in the game; weather/ground conditions; amount of space to perform in; type of music/apparatus selected; spectators; when to apply/adapt/change.

(b) *A good response should include some or most of the points as outlined below. The candidate must demonstrate applied Knowledge and Understanding about the factors considered when selecting a Structures, Strategies and Composition.*

Structures, Strategies and Composition

The candidate must describe in detail the Structure, Strategy or Composition. Some will also make reference possibly to the role they played as well.

These will include:

- fast break/zones/1-3-1/horse shoe offence in basketball/man/man defence
- Football – 4-2-4/4-3-3/3-5-2
- Badminton – front-back-side-side
- Gymnastics particular sequence-routine
- Volleyball – rotation
- Hockey – penalty corner
- Dance – a particular dance or routine used

(c) *A good response should include some or most of the points as outlined below. The candidate must briefly describe a situation where they had to change or adapt their Structures, Strategies and Composition. They must also show critical thinking as to how these changes or adaptations made their performance more effective.*

Evaluate effectiveness

The responses will be wide ranging and will depend on the choice of Structures, Strategies and Composition selected. Responses should start with a description of the problem they faced. They should then show evidence of problem solving and decision making to make their performance more effective. The candidate may decide to change Structures, Strategy and Composition completely. For example:
in basketball we were playing a 2-1-2 zone…opposition had good outside shooters…scored frequently …we changed to half court man/man defence to stop them… this led to less successful shots as they were under more pressure ….forced them to try and drive to basket. They made more mistakes …scored less baskets as they were poor at driving to basket…we won more

turnovers and could attack more.

The candidate may decide to alter the Structures, Strategy and Composition. For example:
in football we played a 4-4-2 formation …we found when attacking all 4 players in midfield would be up the park… supporting the forwards …when the attack broke down the opposition often broke quickly …our midfield were slow to get back…our defence was under pressure …we adapted Structures, Strategies and Composition by having one player…holding in midfield in front of back four …one midfield supporting strikers…and two in middle to move back and forward as necessary…this led to a more balanced attack and defence and allowed us to prevent the opposition breaking quickly … holding midfielder was able to delay attack … allow others to get back.

(d) *A good response should include some or most of the points as outlined below. The candidate must demonstrate applied Knowledge and Understanding about the evaluated improvements to the Structures, Strategy and Composition chosen.*

The responses will include descriptions of particular methods to gather information on effectiveness followed by an explanation. These could include: video/game analysis; observation schedules; Knowledge of Results; criteria checklists; statistics; personal reflection; feedback; internal/external; comparison to previous information gathered; match analysis sheets. For example:
in basketball… we used a criteria checklist… all aspects of fast break… data was collected from a game this then allowed… comparison to previous… to see if we had improved its effectiveness.

HIGHER PHYSICAL EDUCATION 2009

In the Higher Physical Education examination candidates will answer from the perspective of their experiences in a wide variety of activities. An activity specific answer section would result in an enormous document which would be extremely cumbersome and time-consuming to use and which could never realistically cover all possibilities.

In relation to **all** questions it should be noted that the relevance of the content in the candidates' responses will depend on:

- the activity selected
- the performance focus
- the training/development programme/programme of work selected
- the practical experiences of their course as the contexts for answers.

PERFORMANCE APPRECIATION

1. (a) *A good response should include some or most of the points as outlined below.*

   Demands: Technical, Physical, Mental and Special. Candidates may demonstrate acquired Knowledge and Understanding across all related demands or focus on one more comprehensively. Similarly, candidates may demonstrate acquired Knowledge and Understanding in respect of the unique game/event demands or emphasise the demands unique to the role/solo/duo performance relative to the activity selected.

   Special Performance Qualities: The responses will be wide ranging and relevant to the activity selected. Candidates may demonstrate acquired Knowledge and Understanding in respect of the specific role/solo related demands necessary for an effective performance.

   Reference to the application of a series of complex skills will impact on performance in competitive situations. For example:

   in relation to **role demands**,... *as a central defender I am pushed to my limits in the later stages of the game... it is essential that I time my tackles or I will give away penalties... I need to control the ball artistically to wrong foot my opponent and get the ball out of danger areas... etc*

   in relation to **solo demands**... *as a gymnast I know that my tumbling routine has many complex skills that need to be performed in a linked sequence... I need tremendous focus as often I will be pushing myself to the limits... etc... most importantly I need to add flair and fluency in my routine to attract the best marks from the judges... etc.*

   Candidates, who are elite performers may demonstrate acquired Knowledge and Understanding in respect of the application of strategy/composition at appropriate times to ensure an effective performance. Often this link is made in cognisance of Knowledge of Performance and or Knowledge of Results. For example: *reflecting on previous performances we knew to double mark their key player as this would... etc... by applying a man to man strategy immediately would effectively tire them out and give us an advantage... etc... reflecting on my previous results I had to decide which solo piece to execute that would attract the best marks from the judges... etc.*

   (b) *A good response should include some or most of the points as outlined below. To demonstrate acquired Knowledge and Understanding the candidate's response should include descriptive detail about their personal performance.*

   Qualities: In relation to **any** of the qualities selected a detailed personal description should be offered. In this respect the candidate may elect to answer from the viewpoint of having a positive or negative effect on performance. Similarly the description could be offered *via* a synopsis of strengths and weaknesses **or** strengths only **or** a comparative synopsis v a model performer.

   For example, candidates may demonstrate acquired Knowledge and Understanding in respect of the:

   Technical Qualities: Reference may be made to a wide repertoire of skills eg *my dribbling, passing shooting etc is consistent and accurate*; this may be accompanied by clarification of success rate/quality of execution of preparation, action, recovery. For example, *like a model performer I execute my... with power etc.*

   Reference may also be made to the classification of skills demanded, for example, simple/complex etc.

   Physical Qualities: Reference may be made to more than one aspect of fitness. To support acquired/applied Knowledge and Understanding the candidate must describe how the selected aspect of fitness affected performance. For example, my high levels of **Cardio Respiratory Endurance**, **Speed End** *helped me maintain pace and track my opponents continuously ... etc ... my poor flexibility makes it difficult for me to... etc ... Unlike a model performer my lack of power meant that... etc.*

   Personal Qualities: Reference may be made to inherent qualities, for example, **height** – *helped me to win rebounds consistently*, Other acceptable personal qualities such as being decisive/determined/confident/competitive etc, *put me at an advantage and intimidated my opponents... etc.*

   Special Qualities: Reference may be made to the ability to create opportunity, disguise intent, make performance look more dynamic, apply flair, have the ability to choreograph routines/link complex skills... etc. For example, *these unique qualities helped me to fake my intent and so wrong foot my opponent/my routine was exciting to watch...* **or** *this helped me gain points etc.*

   (c) *A good response should include some or most of the points as outlined below. The candidate should demonstrate acquired and applied Knowledge and Understanding in the discussion of the programme considering both strengths and development needs.*

   ### Organising of training
   Within the response examples should include:
   Knowledge of previously stated strengths and weaknesses. Setting of objectives/preparation for competitive event.

   Decisions taken as a result of the performance weaknesses/ strengths reflective of appropriate training/development method(s) and or selected training regimes.
   Training considerations offered should reflect and offer examples based on the: complexity of identified weaknesses, stage of learning, complexity of stacks etc.

   Training considerations may include some or more of the following: training in/out of the activity/conditioning approach, integrated training.

   (d) *A good response should include some or most of the points as outlined below.*

   ### The importance of monitoring and reviewing
   A good response will highlight the differences/benefits of the purpose of monitoring = ongoing process. Such as – reference to appropriate data methods to facilitate

comparison of improvements, achieving targets set, gaining and acting on feedback, aids motivation, ensures further challenge and progress.

Importantly, the response must include reference to reviewing performance = summative progress. Many candidates will repeat or include some of the previously mentioned comments. However reference to the evaluation of the **whole** process ie the impact of the training/development programme/programme of work should be highlighted. Judgements on the success/effectiveness of the programme/ used **plus** judgements on the success/effectiveness to whole performance must be clearly defined.

2. (a) *A good response should include some or most of the points as outlined below. The candidate should demonstrate a level of critical thinking when considering the study of model performance.*

The use of Model performance
A good response will include reference to the impact on learning and/or developing a specific part of their performance. Most likely this will pertain to skill learning/ development. For example, using a model performer can advantage performance or developmental process in a number of ways.

- Identifies strengths and weaknesses.
- Increases confidence, motivation.
- Provides various types of feedback; qualitative, quantitive, diagnostic etc.
- Provides challenge in practice/competition.
- Provides accurate feeds continuously.
- Inspires to achieve higher levels of achievement.
- Supports planning practices/targets.
- Inspires to copy ideas.

For example: *I watched model performers in my class... I was inspired by them and wanted to be as good as they were... When perfecting my right hand lay-up I got feedback from them and they provided me with 1v1 challenge... this level of direct competition helped as a form of target setting; this kept me motivated and determined to do better... I gained in confidence and felt that my technique had greatly improved as a result... etc.*

(b) *A good response should include some or most of the points as outlined below.*

Model performance comparison
A good response will include reference to the range and qualities that are evident in a model performer's repertoire. Reference may be made across the range of demands required in performance ie technical, physical, skill and mental related.
In relation to the demand selected relevant points may come from both 'like/unlike' perspective. For example; *unlike a model performer I do not have a repertoire of skills to meet the technical demands of... I fail to execute my... at the correct time and lack consistency, fluency. Unlike the model performer I look clumsy and lack economy of movement... they make everything look so effortless... their movements/application of skills are used at the right time. However like the model performer I can manage my emotions, I rarely display bad temper and concentrate fully on my game/role ... etc.*

(c) *A good response should include some or most of the points as outlined below.*

Course of action
A good response will include adequate details relevant to the selection and appropriateness of the **most** relevant methods of practice/development/training available.

Considerations of different methods will be evident in the process. Examples relevant to selected methods and how this will bring about improvement more commensurate to a model performer must be evident.
For example, *to make sure my lay-up shot was more like a model performer. At first I used many repetition drills in a closed environment to ensure I had no pressure... etc. I then progressed to more open practice and used combination/conditioned drills to ensure refinement of shot ie against opposition I was more efficient, accurate.*

A link to other relevant factors may include; whole part, gradual build up, problem solving contexts etc. A good response may typically include other relevant factors to demonstrate Knowledge and Understanding such as, progression, feedback, target setting, work to rest considerations, Stages of Learning, complexity of technique being developed, factors affecting performance, principles of effective practice.

(d) *A good response should include some or most of the points as outlined below.*

Course effectiveness/impact on performance development
A good response **must** include evaluative comments and offer detailed examples on how and why they thought the course of action taken was effective, for example, *As I practised in both closed and open contexts this helped me to practise with and without pressure... this helped me to gain confidence before... etc.*
The student should elaborate by stating the impact of skill/technique development to **whole** performance development. For example, a more consistent shooter with higher shooting average/more points won, a positive benefit including greater confidence/better help to team etc.

PREPARATION OF THE BODY

3. (a) *A good response should include some or most of the points as outlined below. The candidate's response should include detail from method(s) used within and outwith the activity.*

Accurate collection and recording of data
Gathering data– The description of the method could be within the activity. A diagram may feature in the answer, for example, a time related observation schedule within football, showing information relevant to the particular aspect selected which was speed end/Cardio Respiratory Endurance. In the answer the candidate should make reference to the processes used to gather information. A narrative account of what was done and ***why*** should be obvious showing logical thinking. Methods could include video/performance profiles/checklists/ scattergrams/Preparation, Action, Recovery/stroke counts/breath counts/pulse counts/feedback - reliability and validity of method should be apparent.

Methods could come from outwith activity. For example, Standardised tests will also be described, these could include:

Physical – 12 minute Cooper test, Sit and reach test, Harvard step test, Bleep test

Skill related – Illinois agility test, ruler drop, alternative hand throw

Mental – questionnaires or self evaluation tests, internal/ external feedback.

(b) *A good response should include some or most of the points as outlined below. The reasons outlined should be justified.*

Importance of analysing and interpreting results for preparation and monitoring of training programmes

The responses will include the results arising from the information gathered and could include reference to specific fitness demands for the activity or perhaps the role within the activity. Reference should be made to the importance of analysing and interpretation of results. This allows the candidate to establish pre training fitness levels and what they need to work on making specific reference to their strengths and weaknesses in terms of fitness. It also provides a bench mark to work on. Specific and realistic targets can be set over a planned period of time. It also allows for the planning of a relevant training programme applying the principles of training. Knowledge of fitness levels before training allows comparison to be carried out with post training results. This also allows monitoring to take place to see if the selected training programme has been successfully managed and carried out.

(c) *A good response should include some or most of the points as outlined below. The candidate must demonstrate both acquired and applied Knowledge and Understanding with regards to principles of training.*

Principles of training

The answer must refer to the principles of training. Most of the following principles should be referred to: specificity to activity/person/performance – progressive overload – frequency – intensity – duration – adaptation – rest/recovery/over training/reversibility.

You will probably have detail or description of how they were applied to programme and also explanation and justification why they were considered.

For example:
I made sure the training was specific to the weakness identified… also demands of activity… I trained 3 times per week with rest every other… allowed body to recover… applied overload after week 3… increased number of sets… training became harder and body adapted to new load… as I was getting fitter… variety within programme… prevent boredom and keep motivation high.

(d) *A good response should include some or most of the points as outlined below. The candidate must demonstrate relevant Knowledge and Understanding and show critical thinking about the impact of training on whole performance.*

The evaluating process

A good response will show knowledge about the purpose and importance of the process. It may provide qualitative or quantitative details of whether the training is effective/working – it can substantiate the specific fitness progress – explanations may include/provide evidence to compare progress/targets/improvements – enables changes to be made – ensure future targets – further challenges – promotes motivation – whether training method was appropriate – deciding if training was at correct intensity – whether short term or long term goals had been achieved.

Impact on performance

For example:
during my basketball game my improved level of Cardio Respiratory Endurance… allowed me to keep up with my player even in later stages of the game… I was still able to get back quickly to defend… was able to maintain a high level of performance throughout the game.
The evidence must relate to the whole performance, with relevant answers given.

4. (a) *A good response should include some or most of the points as outlined below. The candidate must demonstrate acquired Knowledge and Understanding in the description of how one*

skill related and one physical aspect of fitness contributes to effective performance within the selected activity.

Physical skill related and mental types of fitness: You would expect the candidate to select the most appropriate type or more than one aspect within that type to show relevant Knowledge and Understanding to support the answer.

Physical fitness: Cardio Respiratory Endurance – speed – muscular endurance – flexibility – stamina – strength – aerobic/anaerobic endurance – speed endurance – power.

Skill related fitness: reaction time – agility – co-ordination – balance – timing – movement anticipation.

Mental fitness: level of arousal – rehearsal – managing emotion – visualisation – motivation – determination – anxiety – managing stress – concentration.

All responses should make reference to how the types or aspect(s) chosen relate to **effective** performance in the activity.

Physical fitness: For example: *in football a high level of Cardio Respiratory Endurance and speed endurance allowed me to track and help my defence out… as well as support the attackers… throughout the whole game… also having good strength as a defender allowed me to jump and challenge for high balls and crosses… and win tackles against the opposition.*

Skill related fitness: For example: *in badminton having good agility will allow me quick movement… to reach the shuttle or change direction if necessary and return the shuttle to put my opponent under pressure – also… good timing will allow me to connect with the shuttle in the correct place and allow me to execute the shot correctly… hopefully leading to a successful outcome.*

Mental fitness: For example: *in basketball as the ball carrier, by managing my emotions, I was able to handle the pressure my opponent was putting on me when closely marking… I was able to make the correct decision and carry out the correct pass to my team mate successfully… also, when I was taking a free throw, by managing my emotions and rehearsing my routine in my mind… I was able to execute the free throw successfully.*

(b) *A good response should include some or most of the points as outlined below. The candidate must demonstrate acquired knowledge in the description of a method of training and detailed discussion of the advantages of using the method.*

Appropriate methods of training to improve physical/skill related and mental fitness

The candidates responses will be wide ranging and depend on the choice of activity and the type or aspect of fitness selected. Various methods of training could be chosen and some candidates may choose one session or a block of time to describe what they did. Training could be within activity/outwith/combination and involve some of the following methods – fartlek/continuous/conditioning/interval/circuit/weight training/relaxation/breathing/rehearsal.

For example:
I used interval training for swimming… warm up of 8 lengths multi stroke… then some stroke improvement… then main set… 6 × 50 metre swim with a minute rest between each set… then sub set…
6 × 50… 45 second recovery. This was appropriate because it enables high intensity work combined with rest to allow me to train for a longer period of time and thus gaining greater benefits from training.

(c) *A good response should include some or most of the points as outlined below. The candidate must demonstrate acquired knowledge in the description of a method of training and detailed discussion of the advantages of using the method.*

Appropriate methods of training to improve physical/skill related and mental fitness

The candidates responses will be wide ranging and depend on the choice of activity and the type or aspect of fitness selected. Various methods of training could be chosen and some candidates may choose one session or a block of time to describe what they did. Training could be within activity/outwith/combination and involve some of the following methods –fartlek/continuous/conditioning/interval/circuit/weight training/relaxation/breathing/rehearsal.

For example:
For skill related fitness to improve my agility in basketball… I used a circuit… a group of exercises designed for agility… dribbling in and out of cones… I did each exercise for 45 seconds and did 3 sets.

(d) *A good response should include some or most of the points as outlined below.*

The importance of monitoring and reviewing

A good response will show knowledge about the purpose and importance of the process. It may provide qualitative or quantitative details of whether the training is effective/working – it can substantiate the specific fitness progress – explanations may include/provide evidence to compare progress/targets/improvements – enables changes to be made – ensure future targets/further challenges – promotes motivation – whether training method was appropriate – deciding if training was at correct intensity – whether short term or long term goals had been achieved.

SKILLS AND TECHNIQUES

5. (a) *A good response should include some or most of the points as outlined below.*

Appropriate methods of data collection

Description of method(s) used must be offered; a diagram will often feature to support answer. The appropriateness of the methods described should enable either qualitative or quantitative details of performance progress. A range of relevant methods will be selected from: movement/mechanical or consideration of quality.

In context of the answer candidates should reference the *'process'* ie **how** the data was collected. A narrative account of *what* was done and *why* should be obvious; thus demonstrating logical thinking. *Whole* performance skills/fitness/qualities may be gathered via reliable methods such as video, performance profiles, scattergrams, Match Analysis Sheet, fitness tests etc.

A good response will include reference to whole performance (initial data) and specific (focussed data). To substantiate claims reference should be made to one or more of the following:

Movement Analysis (Observation checklist, Match Analysis sheet)

Preparation/Action/Recovery: Mechanical Analysis of force, levers, propulsion etc

Consideration of Quality: reflecting on whether your skill or technique was controlled/fluent or fast/slow?

Video: Comparison of your performance with that of a model performer. The video allowed playback, freeze frame.

Questionnaire: Questions should be relevant to and have responses such as 'done well', 'needs improvement' or mark your performance on a graded scale.

For example:
by looking at my video performance I identified my performance strengths as… etc… I then selected an observation sheet to look more closely at… etc.

(b) *A good response should include some or most of the points as outlined below. The responses will be wide ranging and relevant to the activity selected but points raised should be justified. Candidates must demonstrate acquired Knowledge and Understanding relevant to the appropriateness of the method selected.*

Identification of performance strengths and weaknesses

The candidate may reflect the comparison to that of a model performer or may reflect a statistical % of success rate when performing. Irrespective of the tack taken, the candidate must demonstrate critical thinking by offering a degree of authenticity in their analysis, crucially this must be substantiated when referenced to the methods used in part (a).

Importantly, the candidate must emphasise how their whole performance was affected. For example:
my inaccurate shooting meant that I… this in turn affected my confidence and execution of other skills… looking at my scattergram I had a high % of shots landing… a poor preparation phase in my smash meant that I was not behind the shuttle when hitting it… this caused me to lose power… etc. A link to other factors such as reduced confidence, affected other parts of game/performance may be evident.

(c) *A good response should include some or most of the points as outlined below. Candidate response should demonstrate Knowledge and Understanding relating to HOW a programme should be designed. In this context both acquired and applied knowledge is examined.*

Programme of work: Knowledge of stated strength and weakness of selected skill/technique.

A range of appropriate development programmes will be offered and may include details about the complexity of identified weaknesses, stage of learning, complexity of skill/technique etc. The responses offered may include details of weeks 1 & 2, weeks 3 & 4, weeks 5 & 6 etc, with progression being evident.

The content and structure given must be supported by examples from the programme.

For example, *As I was at the cognitive stage, I used many shadow/repetition practices to ensure… etc. At the automatic stage of learning I knew to use more pressure/problem solving drills as these would challenge me more… etc. I found the chosen skill very difficult so decided to use gradual build up as this would … etc. In weeks 1 & 2, I concentrated more on simple drills… in weeks 3 & 4, I progressed to more complex drills such as…etc. This built my confidence as I reached my target of… etc.*

A link to other relevant factors may include; whole part, gradual build up, mass/distributed, closed/open contexts, repetitions, target setting, model performers etc.

The responses offered will be wide ranging and will depend on the candidate's choice of skill/technique identified for development in part (b).

The response must include details of the considerations/critical debate about the selection and appropriateness of the methods of practice/development programme followed. In this respect the candidate should be convincing in their argument about **why** one method was selected in preference to another ie *the 'process' should be obvious and justified.*

(d) *A good response should include some or most of the points as outlined below.*

Whole performance development

A good response will highlight the impact of skill/technique development to WHOLE performance development. For example a more consistent application/less errors/more points won, a positive benefit including greater confidence etc.

The candidate may also include details referencing specific drills or parts of the programme that benefited their performance, for example, I felt that the repetition drills such as… improved my ability to… etc.

Similarly a comparative synopsis via a statistical % comparison before and after, or comparative to a model performer may also feature in the response.

Merit should be given to the feasibility/validity/justification for claims of improved performance.

Reflective, critical thinking must be demonstrated where the candidate examines the actual training programme to question which parts had little or no impact on performance weaknesses. Also, the candidate may choose to focus on another, different weakness which limits performance.

6. (a) *A good response should include some or most of the points as outlined below. The candidate's response should demonstrate critical thinking in the evaluation of highlighted weaknesses to the WHOLE performance.*

Development needs must be described with reference to the WHOLE performance. This may include quantitative evidence, ie the % success rate of specific aspects of performance.

Importantly the candidate must **emphasise** how their whole performance was affected. For example:
my inaccurate shooting meant that I… this in turn affected my confidence and execution of other skills… looking at my scattergram I had a high % of my shots landing… a poor preparation phase in my smash meant that I was not behind the shuttle when hitting it – this caused me to lose power… etc. A link to how other factors such as reduced confidence, affected other parts of game performance may be evident.

(b) *A good response should include some or most of the points as outlined below.*

Practice considerations

A good response will include details relevant to the selection and appropriateness of the MOST relevant methods of practice/development/training available. Considerations of different methods will be evident in the process. Examples relevant to selected methods will be included highlighting the selections made.

For example, at the cognitive stage, many shadow/repetition practices were incorporated to ensure… etc. At the associative stage some shadow/repetition practices progressing to combination drills… etc. At the automatic stage of learning more pressure/problem solving drills were used to advance and challenge learning and performance development.

A link to other relevant factors may include; whole part, gradual build-up, mass/distributed, closed/open contexts etc.

(c) *A good response should include some or most of the points as outlined below. The candidate's response should demonstrate sound Knowledge and Understanding about the principles of effective practice with exemplification of HOW these were applied. In this context both acquired and applied knowledge is examined.*

Principles of effective practice

Often the acronym S.M.A.R.T.E.R. features in the candidate's answer. A good response will include a systematic discussion of each of the principles inclusive of exemplification of how these principles were applied to the programme described in part b). For example, practice should be specific, measurable, attainable, realistic, time related, exciting and regular… *as my programme was specific it helped me to achieve success… I could target the specific part of my technique that needed most improvement. I knew to set targets and raise them once… this ensured my practice was motivating etc.*

Other relevant knowledge will reference to factors such as practice needs to show progression to ensure targets were reached/enabled refinement/remediation/regression as required, increased motivation, improved confidence, consideration of work rest ratio etc.

(d) *A good response should include some or most of the points as outlined below.*

The importance of monitoring and reviewing

A good response will highlight the differences/benefits of the purpose of monitoring = ie the ongoing process. Such as – reference to appropriate data methods to facilitate comparison of improvements, achieving targets set, gaining and acting on feedback, aids motivation, ensures further challenge and progress.

Importantly, the response must include reference to reviewing performance = ie summative process.

Many candidates will repeat or include some of the previously mentioned comments. However reference to the evaluation of the **whole** process ie the impact of the training/development programme/programme of work should be highlighted. Judgements on the success/effectiveness of the programme/used **PLUS** judgements on the success/ effectiveness to whole performance must be clearly defined.

STRUCTURES, STRATEGIES AND COMPOSITIONS

7. (a) *A good response should include some or most of the points as outlined below..*

Recognising the demands of individual roles during performance.

For example:
in basketball as a centre my role was to rebound the ball in offence and block out in defence… shoot close to basket… to link with forwards and guards in passing movements in and around key.

The candidate should give details of the specific responsibilities a particular role demands. This can include attacking, defensive responsibilities or, in a creative environment, decisions a performer might make during a performance to adjust positioning or even timing.

The candidate may also describe a structure, strategy or composition they have performed within, but it is important that their ROLE within this is identified.

The possible structure, strategy or composition might be: fast break/zones/1-3-1/horse shoe offence in basketball/man-man defence

Football 4-2-4/4-3-3/3-5-2
Badminton front - back-side-side
Gymnastics particular sequence - routine
Volleyball - rotation
Hockey penalty corner

(b) *A good response should include some or most of the points as outlined below. Candidate must demonstrate acquired Knowledge and Understanding regarding the features required to achieve success in the role identified.*

Recognising the need to maximise strengths within a structure, strategy or composition

For example, the answers may vary according to the structure, strategy or composition selected. The following factors may be apparent in answers – to use particular players with particular roles – strengths of these players – types of opposition – attack/defence being applied by my team or opposition – time restrictions in game – after a particular time or situation in activity – ground/weather conditions – prior or previous knowledge of opponent(s) previous results.

For example:
Having played against my opponent previously… I knew his backhand was weak, so I made sure I served to that side, this led to a poor return… also I had forced my opponent out wide in service area… led often to me volleying an outright winner.

The strengths identified must relate to the role identified.

For example:
In my role as specialist setter in my volleyball team I had to be able to convert even poor passes into attacking opportunities for my spikers… I had to be able to make quick decisions about where the set was going in order to avoid the block or to give my spikers the opportunity to capitalise on spaces or weaknesses on my opponent's side of the net… I also had to be able to judge what type of set my spikers preferred.

(c) *A good response should include some or most of the points as outlined below.*

The role identified should remain the focus for the programme of work. Either to deal with weaknesses and/or to ensure steady development of the structure, strategy or composition.

The answers might include identification of weakness(es). Some candidates may answer by referring to the weakness(es) as a team or as an individual. They must show critical thinking by offering a degree of authenticity in their analysis and should make reference as to how their whole performance could be affected.

For example:
My backhand volley was poor – made most errors from this technique/usually went into net or out of court – lost many points – poor second serve, often too short – opponents exploit this leading to lost points – exploitation by opponent – passed on many occasions. Also a link to other factors such as reduced confidence, lack of fitness etc may be evident in the answers.

Candidates should show evidence of problem-solving and decision-making to make their performance more effective.

The candidate may decide to alter the responsibilities held within the structure, strategy or composition.

For example: *in football we played a 4-4-2 formation… we found when attacking, all 4 players in midfield would be up the park… supporting the forwards… when the attack broke down the opposition often broke quickly… our midfield were slow to get back… our defence was under pressure… we adapted the structure, strategy or composition by having one player…*

holding in midfield in front of back four… one midfield supporting strikers… and two in middle to move back and forward as necessary… this led to a more balanced attack and defence and allowed us to prevent the opposition breaking quickly. Holding midfielder was able to delay attack… allow others to get back.

(d) *A good response should include some or most of the points as outlined below.*

A good response will highlight the importance of reviewing performance. This will include:
- checking if training is effective/successful in improving performance
- being aware of the different performance situations where structure, strategy or composition might need to change to suit the demands of the performance
- to set new targets/goals for further performance development
- to aid motivation and give new challenges.

8. (a) *A good response should include some or most of the points as outlined below.*

The responses will be wide ranging and will depend on the choice of Structures, Strategy and Composition selected. Responses will include some of the following – strengths and weaknesses of your own team – strengths and weaknesses of the opposition – particular strengths of individual players within the Structures, Strategy and Composition – experience of players in team or opposition – previous results – how long you can apply the Structures, Strategy and Composition – score in the game – time in the game – weather/ground conditions – amount of space to perform in – type of music/apparatus selected – spectators – when to apply/adapt/change – the need to ensure movements match in terms of being in time to the music/being synchronised with others in the group and include an element of improvisation where appropriate.

Individual strengths and weaknesses in a structure, strategy or composition

For example: *in tennis I used a serve volley strategy… I would serve fast and hard to opponent… follow my serve… get into net and position quickly… use a volley to win point… from opponents return.*

My strengths were, I had a consistent and fast first serve… high percentage of being in… quick to get to net… good forehand volley technique… made winners from first volley.

The need to cooperate and support in team or group situations

For example: *in football in 3-5-2- the defenders in the back 3 must cooperate and support one another… if a long ball is played they must make sure they are not square with one another… and too far apart… they can avoid this by talking to one another and moving closer together… or if one goes to ball the other 2 cover across to plug the gaps and support the defender going to ball.*

Identifying and exploiting opponents' weaknesses

For example: *having played against my opponent previously… I knew his backhand was weak… so I made sure I served to that side… this led to a poor return… also I had forced my opponent out wide in service area… led often to me volleying an outright winner.*

Timing precision and improvisation in performance

For example: *my actions in my dance… had to fit precisely with my choice of music… timing had to be exact… my footwork, steps and jumps had to be timed and precise… so I always arrived where I intended to … and for maximum visual impact on the audience.*

(b) *A good response should include some or most of the points as outlined below.*

The advantages may vary according to the structure, strategy or composition selected. The following factors may be apparent in answers – to use particular players with particular roles – strengths of these players – type of opposition – attack/defence being applied by my team or opposition – time restrictions in game – after a particular time or situation in activity – ground/weather conditions – prior or previous knowledge of opponent(s) previous results – amount of space to perform in – type of music or apparatus selected or the presence of spectators.

The advantages should also include reference to the width, depth and mobility of the structure, strategy and the compositional elements which require consideration in creative activities.

The candidate must describe in detail the structure, strategy or composition. Some will also make reference possibly to the role they played as well.
These will include fast break/zones/1-3-1/horse shoe offence in basketball/man-man defence
Football – 4-2-4/4-3-3/3-5-2
Badminton – front-back-side-side
Gymnastics particular sequence – routine
Volleyball – rotation
Hockey – penalty corner
Dance – a particular dance or routine used

For example: *Having played against my opponent previously… I knew his backhand was weak… so I made sure I served to that side… this led to a poor return… also I had forced my opponent out wide in service area… led often to me volleying an outright winner.*

(c) *A good response should include some or most of the points as outlined below.*

The limitations of various systems of play
The responses will be wide ranging and will depend on the choice of Structures, Strategy and Composition selected. Responses should start with a description of the problem they faced. They should then show evidence of problem-solving and decision-making to make their performance more effective. The candidate may decide to change Structures, Strategy and Composition completely.

For example:
in basketball we were playing 2-1-2 zone… opposition had good outside shooters… scored frequently… we change to half court man/man defence to stop them… this led to less successful shots as they were under more pressure… forced them to try and drive to basket. They made more mistakes… scored less baskets as they were poor at driving to basket… we won more turnovers and could attack more.

The candidate may decide to alter the Structures, Strategies and Composition. For example:
in football we played a 4-4-2 formation… we found when attacking, all 4 players in midfield would be up the park… supporting the forwards… when the attack broke down the opposition often broke quickly… our midfield were slow to get back… our defence was under pressure… we adapted Structures, Strategies and Composition by having one player… holding in midfield in front of back four… one midfield supporting strikers… and two in middle to move back and forward as necessary… this led to a more balanced attack and

defence and allowed us to prevent the opposition breaking quickly. Holding midfielder was able to delay attack… allow others to get back.

The course of action taken to minimise the effects of a weakness might include details of a skill development programme for a specific skill. This must be related to the WHOLE performance.

(d) *A good response should include some or most of the points as outlined below.*

Responses must be linked to previous identified weaknesses. Observations should now illustrate the improvements which can be seen in the WHOLE performance.

For example in netball:
I can now see that the centre pass does not break down as the ball is passed to the wing attack near the side line because she is delaying her movement out to the side line, tricking her opponent into thinking she is going to receive the ball near the centre circle. This means that a secure, safe pass is received and the goal attack is able to time her dodge to receive the next pass near the top of the shooting circle. As a result the strategy of using the WA to create a space to allow a penetrating pass through the middle of the court has been successful. This allowed our confidence to increase and we began playing with much more determination and our opponents found it difficult to mark us and anticipate what we were going to do next.

HIGHER PHYSICAL EDUCATION 2010

In the Higher Physical Education examination candidates will answer from the perspective of their experiences in a wide variety of activities. An activity specific answer section would result in an enormous document which would be extremely cumbersome and time-consuming to use and which could never realistically cover all possibilities.

In relation to **all** questions it should be noted that the relevance of the content in the candidates' responses will depend on:

- the activity selected
- the performance focus
- the training/development programme/programme of work selected
- the practical experiences of their course as the contexts for answers.

PERFORMANCE APPRECIATION

1. (a) *A good response should include some or most of the points as outlined below. The candidate's response should demonstrate detailed knowledge of the importance of each.*

    Special Performance Qualities: The responses will be wide ranging and relevant to the activity selected. Candidates may demonstrate acquired Knowledge and Understanding in respect of the specific role/solo related demands necessary for an effective performance.

    Reference to the application of a series of complex skills will impact on performance in competitive situations. For example, in relation to **role demands**,...*as a central defender I am pushed to my limits in the later stages of the game...it is essential that I time my tackles or I will give away penalties...I need to control the ball artistically to wrong foot my opponent and get the ball out of danger areas...etc.*

    In relation to **solo demands**...*as a gymnast I know that my tumbling routine has many complex skills that need to be performed in a linked sequence...I need tremendous focus as often I will be pushing myself to the limits...etc...most importantly I need to add flair and fluency in my routine to attract the best marks from the judges...etc.*

    For example, *in tennis my high level of **accuracy** when placing my second serve enabled me to maintain serving advantage even though my first serve had failed. I was confident that I could place the ball accurately and with the correct amount of spin. This makes it very difficult for my opponent to play a winning return. This had the added advantage of allowing me to be ambitious with my first serve and resulted in me hitting aces. This accuracy was achieved by...Accuracy was also very important when.........*

    (b) *A good response should include some or most of the points as outlined below. The candidate should demonstrate acquired KU and support this with relevant examples.*

    The training programme offered may reflect the development of a technical and skill related quality/demand being developed (or any other relevant combinations). For example, in badminton: the aim = to develop the drop shot WHILST developing improved footwork (agility). The response should include relevant facts; train in the activity using repetition drills – moving to take feeds from right & left hand side of court - combine with footwork drill, eg from T to various numbered areas of court... Progress to combination/conditioned rallies to ensure refinement of shot ie efficiency, accuracy and disguised placement as a result of energy efficient movement to meet the shot with balance and poise to execute the shot and return to base ready for the next shot etc.

    A good response will typically include other relevant factors to demonstrate Knowledge and Understanding such as, progression, model performers, feedback, target setting, work to rest considerations, stages of learning, complexity of technique being developed, factors affecting performance, principles of training and or effective practice.

    (c) *A good response should include some or most of the points as outlined below. The candidate's response should include detailed discussion to demonstrate thorough KU.*

    Setting goals: A good response will highlight the importance of establishing short term goals to help reach longer term goals. Detailed examples should be offered to show understanding about performance gains as a result of setting realistic/attainable goals. For example, ...*inspires/ motivates to do better...lets you see if training is working/needs to be progresses...enables comparisons to be made...is a form of feedback...establishes achievement...can be used to judge performance against success criteria...etc.*

    (d) *A good response should include some or most of the points as outlined below. Detailed description of **more than one** method is required. A maximum mark of 2 will be awarded for a detailed answer on only one method.*

    The importance of monitoring and reviewing: A good response will highlight the differences/benefits of the purpose of monitoring = ongoing process. The candidate may provide qualitative or quantitative details of whether the programme is effective/working, it substantiates specific fitness/skill progress, it makes sure that overload/progressions can be applied as appropriate, etc. Reference to appropriate data methods to facilitate comparison of improvements, enables changes/adaptations to be made during my programme, achieving targets set, gaining and acting on feedback, aids motivation, ensures further challenge and progress. Importantly, the response must include reference to reviewing performance = summative process. Many candidates will repeat or include some of the previously mentioned comments. However reference to the evaluation of the whole process ie the impact of the training/development programme/programme of work should be highlighted. Judgements on the success/effectiveness of the programme/ used PLUS judgements on the success/effectiveness to whole performance must be clearly defined.

2. (a) *A good response should include some or most of the points as outlined below. In discussion the focus should be on how relevant KU was applied "when establishing training priorities"*

    Model performance comparison: A good response will include reference to the range and qualities that are evident in a model performer's repertoire. Reference may be made across the range of demands required in performance ie technical, physical, skill and mental related.

    In relation the demand selected relevant points may come from both 'like/unlike' perspective. For example, *unlike a Model Performer I do not have a repertoire of skills to meet the technical demands of... I fail to execute my...at the correct time and lack consistency, fluency. Unlike the Model Performer I look clumsy by comparison and lack economy of movement...they make everyone look so effortless...their movements/application of skills are used at the right time. However like the Model Performer I can manage my emotions/rarely display bad temper and concentrate fully on my game/role...etc.*

The use of Model performance:

A good response will include reference to the impact on learning and or developing a specific part of their performance. Most likely this will pertain to skill learning/ development. For example, using a model performer can advantage performance or developmental process in a number of ways.

- Identifies strengths and weaknesses.
- Increases confidence, motivation.
- Provides various types of feedback; qualitative, quantitive, diagnostic etc.
- Provides challenge in practice/competition.
- Provides accurate feeds continuously.
- Inspire to achieve higher levels of achievement.
- Supports planning practices/targets.
- Inspires to copy ideas.

For example, *I watched model performers in my class...I was inspired by them and wanted to be as good as they were...When perfecting my right hand lay-up I got feedback from them and they provided me with 1v1 challenge...this level of direct competition helped as a form of target setting; this kept me motivated and determined to do better...I gained in confidence and felt that my technique had greatly improved as a result...I... etc I used.*

(b) *A good response should include some or most of the points as outlined below. The* **specific** *nature of the activity and an* **expansive range** *of demands should be described.*

Nature: Individual/team. The duration of the game/event. The number of player(s)/performers involved. A spectator/ audience event. Indoor/outdoor. Directly/indirectly competitive. Objective/subjective scoring systems in application. Codes of conduct.

Demands: Technical, Physical, Mental and Special. Candidates may demonstrate acquired Knowledge and Understanding across all related demands or focus on one more comprehensively. Similarly, candidates may demonstrate acquired Knowledge and Understanding in respect of the unique game/event demands or emphasise the demands unique to the role/solo/duo performance relative to the activity selected.

Special Performance Qualities: The responses will be wide ranging and relevant to the activity selected. Candidates may demonstrate acquired Knowledge and Understanding in respect of the specific role/solo related demands necessary for an effective performance.

Reference to the application of a series of complex skills will impact on performance in competitive situations. For example, *in relation to role demands,...as a central defender I am pushed to my limits in the later stages of the game...it is essential that I time my tackles or I will give away penalties...I need to control the ball artistically to wrong foot my opponent and get the ball out of danger areas...etc.*
In relation to solo demands...*as a gymnast I know that my tumbling routine has many complex skills that need to be performed in a linked sequence...I need tremendous focus as often I will be pushing myself to the limits...etc...most importantly I need to add flair and fluency in my routine to attract the best marks from the judges...etc.*

Candidates, who are elite performers may demonstrate acquired Knowledge and Understanding in respect of the application of strategy/composition at appropriate times to ensure effective performance. Often this link is made in cognisance of Knowledge of Results and or Knowledge of Performance. For example, *reflecting on previous performances we knew to double mark their key player as this would...etc...by*

applying a man to man strategy immediately would effectively tire them out and give us an advantage... etc...reflecting on my previous results I had to decide which solo piece to execute that would attract the best marks from the judges, etc.

Consideration of activity challenges and qualities demanded

The responses will be wide ranging and relevant to the activity selected. Candidates should demonstrate acquired Knowledge and Understanding in respect of the specific challenges of the activity selected and importantly demonstrate critical thinking by exemplifying the qualities required as a performer to meet the challenges highlighted.

Reference to the type of activity may be evident to set the scene, for example, an individual/team activity, an indoor/outdoor activity, playing competitively or as leisure pursuit will help qualify the candidate's explanations. For example, in relation to activity challenges,...*in squash the challenges I face are demanding...the aim of the game is to get in to the lead with 9 points over my opponent...a win = best out of three games...the challenges requires me to play the ball against at least one wall away from my opponent to gain points without obstructing my opponents route to ball...The qualities I require are skill related – with high levels of agility and reaction time as I...etc. I require high levels of mental skills to ensure I make tactical decisions, patience being crucial as I outmanoeuvre my opponent to take point advantage...*

(c) *A good response should include some or most of the points as outlined below. Candidates may answer in a detailed manner by targeting limited number of areas within physical, technical, personal and special, or they may approach in a broader manner.*

Qualities: In relation to any of the qualities selected a detailed personal description should be offered. In this respect the candidates may elect to answer from the viewpoint of having a positive or negative affect on performance. Similarly the description could be offered via a synopsis of strengths and weaknesses OR strengths only OR a comparative synopsis via a model performer.
For example, candidates may demonstrate acquired Knowledge and Understanding in respect of the:

Technical Qualities: Reference may be made to wide repertoire of skills eg; *my dribbling, passing shooting etc is consistent and accurate; this may be accompanied by clarification of success rate/quality of execution of PAR. For example, like a model performer I execute my...with power etc. Reference may also be made to the classification of skills demanded, for example, simple/complex etc.*

Physical Qualities: Reference may be made to more than one aspect of fitness. To support acquired/applied Knowledge and Understanding the candidates must describe how the selected aspect of fitness affected performance. For example, *my high levels of Cardio Respiratory Endurance, Speed Endurance helped me maintain pace and track my opponents continuously...etc...my poor flexibility makes it difficult for me to...Unlike a Model Performer my lack of power meant that...etc.*

Personal Qualities: Reference may be made to inherent qualities, for example, *height – helped me to win rebounds consistently, Other acceptable personal qualities such as being decisive/determined/confident/competitive etc, put me at an advantage and intimidated my opponents...etc.*

Special Qualities: Reference may be made to the ability to create opportunity, disguise intent, make performance look more dynamic, apply flair, had the ability to choreograph routines/link complex skills... etc. For example, *these* *unique qualities helped me to fake my intent and so wrong foot my opponent/my routine was exciting to watch…OR this helped me gain more points etc.*

(d) *A good response should include some or most of the points as outlined below. Programme of work must link to the selected quality. Detailed discussion on how the programme helped improve overall performance should form basis of answer. Examples should be used to support argument and illustrate points. The candidate may select an isolated or an integrated training approach.*

Course of action: A good response will include adequate details relevant to the selection and appropriateness of the **MOST** relevant methods of practice/development/training available. Considerations of different methods will be evident in the process. Examples relevant to selected methods and how this will bring about improvement more commensurate to model performer must be evident. For example, *to make sure my lay up shot was more like a model performer. At first I used many repetition drills in a closed environment to ensure I had no pressure…etc. I then progressed to more open practice and used combination/conditioned drills to ensure refinement of shot ie against opposition I was more efficient, accurate.*

A link to other relevant factors may include; whole part whole, gradual build up, problem solving contexts etc. A good response may typically include other relevant factors to demonstrate Knowledge and Understanding such as, progression, feedback, target setting, work to rest considerations, stages of learning, complexity of technique being developed, factors affecting performance, principles of effective practice.

Planning implications: The candidate's experiences will dictate the terms of reference used, ie as an individual/team game performer or as an athlete or swimmer's perspective some of the following training terms will most commonly be used; short/long term targets, preseason, competitive season and post season, mini, macro, meso cycles, to train in or out with the activity, the need to ensure peak fitness readiness, periodisation principles.

A good response will demonstrate both acquired and applied Knowledge and Understanding. The candidate must reflect on decisions made about their specific training considerations. In this respect, the link to their identified fitness needs will be highlighted with exemplification of the particular stages of training and types of training used. To ensure training effectiveness related Knowledge and Understanding about training principles/principles of effective practice will most likely be made.

Organising of training: Within the response examples should include:
Cognisance of previously stated Strengths & Weaknesses.
Setting of objectives/preparation for competitive event.

Decisions taken as a result of the performance weaknesses/strengths reflective of appropriate training/development method(s) and or selected training regimes.
Training considerations offered should reflect and offer examples based on the: complexity of identified weaknesses, stage of learning, complexity of task etc.
Training considerations may include some or more of the following: training in/out of the activity/conditioning approach, integrated training.

The importance of integrated training: Typically the notion of more than one type of fitness/demand being developed at the same time. Reasons should be included to exhibit related Knowledge and Understanding.

The training programme offered may reflect the development of a technical and skill related quality/demand being developed (or any other relevant combinations). For example, in badminton: the aim = to develop the drop shot WHILST developing improved footwork (agility). The response should include relevant facts; train in the activity using repetition drills − moving to take feeds from right & left hand side of court − combine with footwork drill, eg from T to various numbered areas of court…Progress to combination/conditioned rallies to ensure refinement of shot ie efficiency, accuracy and disguised placement as a result of energy efficient movement to meet the shot with balance and poise to execute the shot and return to base ready for the next shot etc.

A good response will typically include other relevant factors to demonstrate Knowledge and Understanding such as, progression, model performers, feedback, target setting, work to rest considerations, stages of learning, complexity of technique being developed, factors affecting performance, principles of training and or effective practice.

PREPARATION OF THE BODY

3. (a) *A good response should include some or most of the points as outlined below. The candidate must demonstrate acquired knowledge when discussing the different approaches to training. They may focus on one activity; consider several activities; or apply KU in a generic manner.*

Specific training types: A good response should have good description of the form of training for selected approach.
In the activity (conditioning) − fartlek short sprints and then continuous paced running with specific description of what they did. For example, *in athletics for 800 metre running I did fartlek training…did 8 laps…jogged the straights and ran the bends…done without stopping…then did 6 short 60 metre sprints with a short 20 metre jog leading into each sprint made demand similar to end of actual race.*
Out with activity could include circuit training/weight training with description of what they did/sets/reps/types of exercise. For example, *to improve my Cardio Respiratory Endurance for my role as a midfielder in hockey…I trained out with activity…carried out some circuit training…doing high intensity work…work rest ratio 1:3…doing a series of exercises…step ups…burpees…continuous running…3 sets of exercises…working on each for 45 seconds.*
Combination of both: continuous training in pool/weight training out of pool with appropriate description of each/involve some of the following methods fartlek/continuous/conditioning/interval/circuit/weight training/relaxation/breathing/rehearsal. For example, *in swimming I trained using a combination of training within activity and out with activity…within I used interval training…working on developing both anaerobic and aerobic fitness…did warm up…then stroke improvement…main set 6×50 metre swim one minute recovery…sub set 6×50…45 secs recovery…then warm down…out with pool did a weight training circuit…doing a series of exercises…3 sets of exercises…also some work on stepping machines…rowing machines…to improve Cardio Respiratory Endurance.*

Appropriateness of selected method
Within activity: can involve specific movements and can develop skills as well as fitness − involve demands of the activity − can also simulate the pressure demands of a competitive situation − can also be fun and motivational.
Out-with activity: can develop both general and specific muscle/fitness − easy to do − minimum of equipment needed.

Combination: some of the above reasons but firmly explained why – variety in different methods – motivational – enjoyable.

(b) *A good response should include some or most of the points as outlined below. The candidate must demonstrate KU related to both planning and implementing training.*

The importance of planning and implementing training: Planning could refer to type of activity or level of fitness or role in activity. Goal setting may be referred to types of training may also be referred to for example circuit, interval etc. For example, *I set myself both short term and long term goals...this gave me a target to work towards...they had to be realistic and achievable...they motivated me to do well.*

The answer could refer to the principles of training. Some of the following principles may be referred to – specificity to activity/person/performance – progressive overload – frequency – intensity – duration – adaptation – rest/recovery/over training/reversibility.

You will probably have detail or description of how they were applied to programme and also explanation and justification why they were considered.

(c) *A good response should include some or most of the points as outlined below. Candidates are expected to select one training session from their programme and give a very detailed description. The session described may be very specific to one aspect of fitness or be more general in nature.*

The candidates responses will be wide ranging and depend on the choice of activity and the type or aspect of fitness selected.

For example, *I used interval training for swimming...warm up of 8 lengths multi stroke...then some stroke improvement...then main set...6×50 metre swim with a minute rest between each set...then sub set...6×50...45 sec recovery. This was appropriate because it enables high intensity work combined with rest to allow me to train for a longer period of time and thus gaining greater benefits from training. This was a session to improve speed endurance.*

(d) *A good response should include some or most of the points as outlined below. Candidates should explain in detail how progress was monitored during the training programme.*

The importance of planning and monitoring training using particular methods

Methods used could include video, observation schedules/training diary/logbook, personal evaluation or game analysis.

For example, *I used a training diary...this allowed me to keep a note of my progress...allowed me to see whether my training had been effective...if I had achieved my short term goals...if my training had been set at the correct level...to see if my overall performance had improved.*

4. (a) *A good response should include some or most of the points as outlined below. The candidate must demonstrate KU of each of the types of fitness in relation to their chosen activity.*

Physical skill related and mental types of fitness: You would expect the candidate to select the most appropriate type or more than one aspect within that type to show relevant Knowledge and Understanding to support the answer.

Physical fitness: Cardio Respiratory Endurance – speed – muscular endurance – flexibility – stamina – strength – aerobic/anaerobic endurance – speed endurance – power.

Skill related fitness: reaction time – agility – co-ordination – balance – timing – movement anticipation.

Mental fitness: level of arousal – rehearsal – managing emotion – visualisation – motivation – determination – anxiety/managing stress/ concentration.

All responses should make reference to how the types or aspect(s) chosen relate to **effective** performance in the activity.

Physical fitness: For example, *in football a high level of Cardio Respiratory Endurance and speed endurance allowed me to track and help my defence out...as well as support the attackers...throughout the whole game...also having good strength as a defender allowed me to jump and challenge for high balls and crosses...and win tackles against the opposition.*

Skill related fitness: For example, *in badminton having good agility will allow me quick movement...to reach the shuttle or change direction if necessary and return the shuttle to put my opponent under pressure – also...good timing will allow me to connect with the shuttle in the correct place and allow me to execute the shot correctly...hopefully leading to a successful outcome.*

Mental fitness: For example, *in basketball as the ball carrier by managing my emotions I was able to handle the pressure my opponent was putting on me when closely marking... I was able to make the correct decision and carry out the correct pass to my team mate successfully...when I was also taking a free throw by managing my emotions and rehearsing my routine in my mind...I was able to execute the free throw successfully.*

Relationship between types/aspects of fitness and the development of activity specific fitness

You would expect the candidate to select an appropriate type/aspect of fitness and relate it to the activity selected and show the appropriateness to it.

For example, *in tennis strength and endurance are important...when serving major muscle groups are involved...to produce a strong service action...it is often repeated during a long game...this requires both muscular endurance and strength...this is specific to this movement in tennis.*

(b) *A good response should include some or most of the points as outlined below. The candidate's response should be a detailed description of **one** method.*

The use of video in conjunction with eg an observation schedule can be considered as one of the methods of gathering information. The method selected may be from within or out with activity.

Accurate collection and recording of data
Gathering data: The description of the method could be within the activity. A diagram may feature in the answer for example a time related observation schedule within football showing information relevant to the particular aspect selected which was speed and/Cardio Respiratory Endurance. In the answer the candidate should make reference to the process as to how the information was gathered. A narrative account of what was done and **why** should be obvious showing logical thinking. Methods could include video/performance profiles/checklists/scatter grams/Preparation, Action, Recovery/stroke counts/breath counts/pulse counts/feedback – reliability and validity of method should be apparent. Methods could come from out with activity. For example, Standardised tests will also be described, these could include:
Physical: 12 minute Cooper test, Sit and reach test, Harvard step test, Bleep test
Skill related: Illinois agility test, Ruler drop, Alternate hand throw

Mental: Questionnaires or self evaluation tests, internal/external feedback

(c) *A good response should include some or most of the points as outlined below. Candidates should demonstrate KU of both validity and reliability in relation to their chosen activity and method.*

Appropriateness of methods used

The appropriateness of the methods described should enable either qualitative or quantative information to be gathered. Explanations offered may include, to provide evidence to compare progress/targets/improvements, to provide a permanent record, can be used time and time again, aids motivation, ensures further challenge and progress, information can be gathered at the beginning and end etc, if video is used it can refer to ability to pause, rewind, play over and over again or be used in conjunction with an observation schedule. For standard tests it allows comparison to set national norms for interpretation.

(d) *A good response should include some or most of the points as outlined below. The candidates response should display both acquired and applied KU when discussing the appropriateness of the selected method of training.*

Appropriate methods of training to improve physical/skill related and mental fitness

The candidates response will be wide ranging and depend on the choice of activity and the type or aspect of fitness selected. Various methods of training could be chosen and some candidates may choose a one session or a block of time to describe what they did. Training could be within activity/out with/combination and involve some of the following methods fartlek/continuous/conditioning/interval/circuit/weight training/relaxation/breathing/rehearsal.

A good response should have good description of the form of training.

In the activity (conditioning): fartlek short sprints and then continuous paced running with specific description of what they did. For example, *in athletics for 800 metre running I did fartlek training…did 8 laps…jogged the straights and ran the bends…done without stopping…then did 6 short 60 metre sprints with a short 20 metre jog leading into each sprint made demand similar to end of actual race.*

Out with activity could include circuit training/weight training with description of what they did/sets/reps/types of exercise. For example, *to improve my Cardio Respiratory Endurance for my role as a midfielder in hockey…I trained out with activity…carried out some circuit training…doing high intensity work…work rest ratio 1:3…doing a series of exercises…step ups…burpees…continuous running…3 sets of exercises… working on each for 45 seconds.*

Combination of both: continuous training in pool/weight training out of pool with appropriate description of each/involve some of the following methods fartlek/continuous/conditioning/interval/circuit/weight training/relaxation/breathing/rehearsal. For example, *in swimming I trained using a combination of training within activity and out with activity…within I used interval training…working on developing both anaerobic and aerobic fitness…did warm up…then stroke improvement…main set 6×50 metre swim one minute recovery…sub set 6×50…45 secs recovery…then warm down…out with pool did a weight training circuit…doing a series of exercises…3 sets of exercises…also some work on stepping machines…rowing machines…to improve Cardio Respiratory Endurance.*

Appropriateness of selected method

Within activity: can involve specific movements and can develop skills as well as fitness − involve demands of the activity − can also simulate the pressure demands of a competitive situation − can also be fun and motivational.

Out-with activity: can develop both general and specific muscle/fitness − easy to do − minimum of equipment needed.

Combination: some of the above reasons but firmly explained why − variety in different methods − motivational − enjoyable.

SKILLS & TECHNIQUES

5. (a) *A good response should include some or most of the points as outlined below.*

Information Processing

Relevant description; this may be supported with use of a diagram. The description should include details appropriate to the skill/technique selected.

The 4 stages should appear in sequence order of INPUT via stimuli/senses/instruction/demonstration or feedback offered. DECISION MAKING − action to be taken. OUTPUT via taking appropriate action.

EVALAUTION − what was the outcome of action taken; successful/unsuccessful, effective/ineffective.

Remediation process now occurs − repeat the action to develop/refine − regress to address weaknesses identified − progress to the next stage.

Skill classification

Relevant description of various types of skill. The description should include details appropriate to the skills selected inclusive of example. The classified skills likely to appear: Open/Closed. Discrete/Serial/Continuous. Simple/Complex.

Points highlighted:

Open − dependent on different variables, externally paced eg a corner kick in football.

Closed − Internally paced, no clear beginning or ending, eg a drive in golf.

Discrete − clear beginning and end, requiring fine motor skills.

Serial − a combination of discrete skills which performed in sequence produces a unique skill such as lay up in Basketball.

Continuous − no clear pattern of beginning or end such as swimming.

Simple − requiring few sub routines, no element of danger = forward roll in gymnastics.

Complex − many sub routines, element of danger = front somersault in gymnastics.

(b) *A good response should include some or most of the points as outlined below.*

Features of a skilled performance

A good response will include reference to the range and qualities that are evident in a skilled/model performance. Reference should be made across the range of qualities displayed ie technical, physical, skill and mental related. A link to other relevant factors may include; wide repertoire of skills evident and executed at the correct time with consistency, fluency, ease of economy. Movements/application of skills seem effortless. Management of emotions are controlled. A degree of confidence. Few unforced errors. Makes appropriate decisions when under pressure etc.

(c) *A good response should include some or most of the points as outlined below. More than 1 method of practice must be mentioned in the programme of work.*

Programme of work: The responses offered will be wide ranging and will depend on the candidate's choice of skill/technique identified for development.

The response may include details of the considerations/critical debate about the selection and appropriateness of the methods of practice/development programme followed. In this respect the candidate should be convincing in their argument about why one method was selected in preference to another ie the 'process' should be obvious and justified.

Programme references may include details of weeks 1 & 2, weeks 3 & 4, weeks 5 & 6, etc OR *I used a gradual build up/whole part whole approach to my development programme.* In this respect the notion of reliability/validity should be apparent and justified etc.

The content and structure given may be justified with progressions exemplified to demonstrate sound Knowledge and Understanding. For example, *as I was at the cognitive stage – I used many shadow/repetition practices to ensure…etc. At the associative stage I used some shadow/repetition practices progressing to combination drills…etc. At the automatic stage of learning I knew to use more pressure/problem solving drills as these would challenge me more…etc. I found the skill very difficult so decided to use gradual build up as this would…etc…In weeks 1 & 2, I concentrated more on simple drills…in weeks 3-4, I progressed to more complex drills such as…etc this built my confidence as I reached my target of…etc.* A link to other relevant factors may include; whole part, gradual build up, mass/distributed, closed/open contexts, repetitions, target setting, model performers etc.

(d) *A good response should include some or most of the points as outlined below.*

The importance of monitoring and reviewing: A good response will highlight the differences/benefits of the purpose of monitoring = ie the ongoing process. Such as – reference to appropriate data methods to facilitate comparison of improvements, achieving targets set, gaining and acting on feedback, aids motivation, ensures further challenge and progress.

Importantly, the response must include reference to reviewing performance = ie summative progress.

Many candidates will repeat or include some of the previously mentioned comments. However reference to the evaluation of the whole process ie the impact of the training/development programme/programme of work should be highlighted. Judgements on the success/effectiveness of the programme/used PLUS judgements on the success/effectiveness to whole performance must be clearly defined.

A good response will highlight the impact of skill technique development to WHOLE performance development. For example, *a more consistent application/less errors/more points won, a positive benefit including greater confidence etc.*

6. (a) *A good response should include some or most of the points as outlined below.*

Stages of learning: A good response will include specific reference and detail appropriate with detailed explanations relevant to the stage of learning described.
Examples are often included to highlight their understanding in context; this may be generic or linked to a specific skill/technique.

For example, at the cognitive stage a performer will be reliant on a lot of instruction/feedback. The performer is learning about the sub routines of the skill/technique. Success rate/effectiveness is not refined etc.

At the associative stage, a performer will still be reliant on instruction/feedback but will be developing ability to self evaluate. The performer is more able to link the sub routines of the skill/technique; the execution of the skill is recognisable but the success rate/effectiveness is still not consistent or highly effective etc.

At the automatic stage, a performer will be less reliant on instruction/feedback with an ability to self evaluate and identify weaknesses. The performer is able to link the sub routines of the skill/technique; the execution of the skill is recognisable with control and consistency etc.

A link to other relevant factors may include; progressions possible from one stage to the next, model/skilled performer etc.

(b) *A good response should include some or most of the points as outlined below.*

Programme of work: The responses offered will be wide ranging and will depend on the candidate's choice of skill/technique identified for development.

The response must include details of the considerations/critical debate about the selection and appropriateness of the methods of practice/development programme followed. In this respect the candidate should be convincing in their argument about why one method was selected in preference to another ie the 'process' should be obvious and justified.
The programme followed should be detailed with reference made to the stage of learning and some of the following considerations: skill complexity classification, Model Performer, feedback, goal setting…etc.

For example, at the cognitive stage – many shadow/repetition practices were incorporated to ensure…etc.
At the associative stage some shadow/repetition practices progressing to combination drills, etc. At the automatic stage of learning more pressure/
problem solving drills were used to advance and challenge learning and performance development.
A link to other relevant factors may include; whole part, gradual build up, mass/distributed, closed/open contexts etc.

(c) *A good response should include some or most of the points as outlined below.*

Motivation/Concentration/Feedback
In this respect the candidate may give a detailed synopsis of how each factor selected impacted upon their learning and or their application of skill/technique. Merit should be given according to depth/quality/relevance of explanations offered. NOTE – it is likely that similar points may be referenced/exemplified in relation to discrete factor.

Motivation = A good response will include details of being internally (intrinsic)/externally (extrinsic) motivated to learn/achieve success. Being motivated enables the performer to be self driven to listen to instruction and act on it, it helps the performer to be self determined/give off their best/come from behind/respond to immediate problems/competitive challenges/not worry if mistakes are made and re channel focus.

Concentration = A good response will include details of the need to concentrate/focus on instruction/demonstration offered to ensure effective execution/application of skill or technique, promotes progression/adaptation of skill or technique, ensures bad habits are not formed/eradicated, enables the performer to perform their role and apply their skills appropriately, promotes the ability to read play/make effective decisions/adapt to the immediate situation…etc. In the context of games, concentration enables the performer to stick to role related duties/application of structure/strategy/game plan…etc.

Feedback = A good response will include details of receiving internal (kinaesthetic) feedback to progress/refine skill or technique OR receiving/giving external feedback (visual/verbal/written/vestibular), to progress/refine skill or technique of self or that of others.
Feedback should be positive/immediate to promote confidence/success.

NOTE A link to Stage of Learning, Model Performers may be made in reference to any of the above factors.

(d) *A good response should include some or most of the points as outlined below.*

Whole performance development
The responses offered will be wide ranging however a good response will highlight the impact of improved skill/technique development to WHOLE performance effectiveness. For example a more consistent application/less errors/more points won, a positive benefit including greater confidence etc.

The candidate may also include details referencing specific drills or parts of the programme that benefited their performance, for example, I felt that the repetition drills such as ????…improved my ability to ???? etc. Similarly a comparative synopis via a statistical % comparison before & after, or comparative to a Model Performer may also feature in the response.

Merit should be given to the feasibility/validity/justification for claims of improved performance.

STRUCTURES, STRATEGIES AND COMPOSITION

7. (a) *A good response should include some or most of the points as outlined below.*

    ### Select a relevant structure, strategy or composition
    The candidate must describe the Structure, Strategy or Composition. Some will also make reference possibly to the role they played as well.
    These will include fast break/zones/1-3-1/horse shoe offence in basketball/man/man defence
    Football – 4-2-4/4-3-3/3-5-2
    Badminton – front-back-side-side
    Gymnastics particular sequence – routine
    Tennis – serve-volley
    Volleyball – rotation
    Hockey – penalty corner

    For example, *in tennis I used a serve volley strategy – I would serve fast and hard to opponent – follow my serve – get into net and position quickly – use a volley to win point – from opponents return.*

    (b) *A good response should include some or most of the points as outlined below.*

    ### Structure and strategy fundamentals
    The following may be referred to or listed.
    Using space in attack and defence, pressuring opponents, tempo of play, speed in attack, delay in defence and principles of play (width, depth and mobility).
    The importance should be justified and show both acquired and applied knowledge.

For example, *in basketball I wanted to play a fast tempo game…attack quickly…so I made sure that on each opportunity we tried to play a fast break…to catch the defence out…score a quick basket…create an overload situation…before the defence was organised properly.*

Structure and compositional fundamentals
The following may be referred to or listed.
Design form, developing motifs, using repetition, variation and contrast, interpreting stimulus in developing performance, using space effectively, using creativity in performance.
The importance should be justified and show both acquired and applied knowledge.
For example, *in dance I started with a simple step motif…took me forwards then back to starting position…then sideways…back to starting…I established this as a simple core motif…then I developed a second core motif…this time a jumping pattern…then I began to mix and play with both core motifs…to add interest to my dance…gave my dance variety and quality of movement contrasts.*

(c) *A good response should include some or most of the points as outlined below.*
The responses will be wide ranging and will depend on the choice of structure, strategy or composition selected. Responses should start with a description of the problem they faced.
For example, *opposition had good outside shooters…scored frequently…we found when attacking all 4 players in midfield would be up the park…supporting the forwards…when the attack broke down the opposition often broke quickly…our midfield were slow to get back…our defence was under pressure.*

(d) *A good response should include some or most of the points as outlined below. Answer should demonstrate critical thinking and decision making in the justification of any changes/adaptations or in the training programme which was organised to overcome the problems faced.*

The importance of adapting and refining a structure, strategy or composition in response to performance demands
The responses will be wide ranging and will depend on the choice of structure, strategy or composition selected. Responses may repeat the description of the problem they faced. They should then show evidence of problem solving and decision making to make their performance more effective. The candidate may decide to change structure, strategy or composition completely. For example, *in basketball we were playing a 2-1-2 zone…opposition had good outside shooters…scored frequently…we changed to half court man/man defence to stop them…this led to less successful shots as they were under more pressure…forced them to try and drive to basket. They made more mistakes…scored less baskets as they were poor at driving to basket…we won more turnovers and could attack more.*

8. (a) (i) *A good response should include some or most of the points as outlined below.*

    Some candidates may answer by referring to the strengths as a team or strengths of the individual.

    Eg…*in tennis I used a serve, volley strategy. As I had a consistent, fast first serve, I would serve fast and hard to my opponent, follow my serve into the net, positioning quickly in order to capitalise on my opponent's weak return.*

An explanation of the impact of this strength on the whole performance must be given eg *My strength allowed me to dictate the rally from the first stroke. I took control of the front court area, dominating the court, putting my opponent under pressure immediately, inevitably winning many points easily in my service game.*

(ii) *A good response should include some or most of the points as outlined below.*

Some candidates may answer by referring to the strengths as a team or strengths of the individual.

Candidates must show critical thinking by offering a degree of authenticity in their analysis and must make reference as to how their WHOLE performance was affected by the weakness, eg …

My backhand volley was poor – made most errors from this technique – usually went into net or out of court – lost many points – poor second serve – often too short – opponents exploit this leading to lost points – exploitation by opponent – passed on many occasions. (Also a link to other factors such as reduced confidence, lack of fitness etc may be evident in answers).

(b) *A good response should include some or most of the points as outlined below.*

Weakness addressed: The responses offered will be wide ranging and will depend on the choice of SSTC selected and the weakness(es) identified. The responses could be a description of the programme of work followed but this must be relevant to weakness mentioned. For example, *for my backhand volley I carried out a skill development programme…partner threw me a ball…play a backhand volley…gradually increased speed and distance…added more pressure…eventually to full speed…then aim for targets on court…two feeders drive me the ball from back of court…alternative backhand/forehand volley…serve to partner and get them to return to backhand side to play volley.* Various methods of training/practice may be described – reference may be made to possible changes to SSTC either as individuals or as part of a team…a range of development programmes will be evident – the structure should be evident as well as the content – the SSTC may be changed or adapted to overcome weakness(es)…substitute player. Responses must show critical thinking and relevant decision making and should reduce the effect of weakness(es) on performance.

(c) *A good response should include some or most of the points as outlined below.*

The responses will include descriptions of particular methods to gather information on effectiveness followed by an explanation – these could include video-game analysis – observation schedules – knowledge of results – criteria checklists – statistics – personal reflection - feedback – internal/external – comparison to previous information gathered - match analysis sheets. For example, *in basketball…we used a criteria checklist…all aspects of fast break…data was collected from a game this then allowed… …comparison to previous…to see if we had improved its effectiveness.*

(d) *A good response should include some or most of the points as outlined below.*

Structure and strategy fundamentals
Using space in attack and defence, pressuring opponents, tempo of play, speed in attack, delay in defence and principles of play (width, depth and mobility).

The importance should be justified and show both acquired and applied knowledge.
For example, *in basketball I wanted to play a fast tempo game…attack quickly…so I made sure that on each opportunity we tried to play a fast break…to catch the defence out…score a quick basket…create an overload situation…before the defence was organised properly.*

Structure and compositional fundamentals
Design form, developing motifs, using repetition, variation and contrast, interpreting stimulus in developing performance, using space effectively, using creativity in performance.
The importance should be justified and show both acquired and applied knowledge.
For example, *in dance I started with a simple step motif…took me forwards then back to starting position…then sideways…back to starting…I established this as a simple core motif…then I developed a second motif…this time a jumping pattern…then I began to mix and play with both core motifs…to add interest to my dance…gave my dance variety and quality of movement contrasts.*

HIGHER PHYSICAL EDUCATION 2011

In the Higher Physical Education examination candidates will have answered from the perspective of their experiences in a wide variety of activities. To produce an activity specific marking scheme would result in an enormous document which would be extremely cumbersome and time-consuming to use and which could never realistically cover all possibilities.

In relation to **all** questions it should be noted that the relevance of the content in the candidates' responses will depend on:

- the activity selected
- the performance focus
- the training/development programme/programme of work selected
- the practical experiences of their course as the contexts for answers.

PERFORMANCE APPRECIATION

1. (a) **Model Performance**

The response may focus on the student's strengths and weaknesses in comparison to model performance.

Reference could be made to a range of qualities:
- Technical
- Physical
- Personal
- Special

For example, *unlike a model performer I do not have a repertoire of skills to meet the technical demands…I fail to execute my…at the correct time and lack consistency, fluency. Unlike the model performer I took clumsy and lack economy of movement…they make everything look effortless…their movements/application of skills are used at the right time. However, like the model performer, I can manage my emotions… I rarely display bad temper and concentrate fully on my game/role.*

(b) **Performance qualities**

The student should select **ONE** quality. The response should focus on how components of this quality were improved over a number of sessions.

It is important that the student is able to describe the actual programme of work used to improve the selected quality.

For example…*to develop my technical ability in badminton I initially worked on my overhead clear and my net shot in isolation…I did this by using feeder practices…I focused on my movement to the shot and my recovery back to base…I then moved to make use of pressure drills and conditioned games…*

(c) **Performance Strengths**

The response should focus on how strengths within the selected quality were utilised in whole performance.

For example…*physical quality…in football…Being powerful enabled me to win more headers and compete in tackles…being strong helped me hold off defenders when I was in possession of the ball…being fast enabled me to run into space to receive a pass.*

(d) **Evaluating performance**

The response should focus on reviewing as a summative process. Reference should be made to some of the following:
- Achieving goals
- Motivational effects
- Setting new targets
- Appropriateness of course of action
- Success of training programme
- Comparing whole performance before and after training

For example…*I compared my performance when playing badminton before training to see if I had improved the effectiveness and consistency (technical qualities) of my overhead shots in the game.*

The response must also focus on giving a clear description of method(s) used to evaluate overall performance following programme of work.

For example…*match analysis, video of whole performance.*

2. (a) **Nature of performance**

The response should focus on the following:
- Individual/team
- Duration of event
- Number of participants
- Environment (indoor/outdoor)
- Directly/indirectly competitive
- Scoring system
- Rules
- Codes of conduct
- Spectators/audience

For example…*in a tennis game there can be 2 players (single) or 4 players (doubles)…a game can last 3 sets or 5 sets. A women's game last for 3 sets. The winner is the person who is the first to achieve 2 sets…the winner of the set has to win by more than one game…if a set is tied at 6 all…a tie break follows…*

(b) **Mental preparation**

The response should give a clear description of how the performer prepared mentally for performance.

Reference may be made to the following.
- Deep breathing
- Mental rehearsal
- Visualisation
- Trigger words
- Meditation
- Self talk

For example…*to enable me to control my anxiety prior to performing my gymnastics routine…I used visualisation to picture myself completing my floor routine successfully…this let me see myself going through all the parts…linking together…landing securely.*

(c) **Integrated training**

The response should describe in detail an integrated programme that developed a variety of the following aspects:
- Physical (preparation of the body)
- Technical (skills and techniques)
- Personal (motivation and personal goals)
- Special (achieving peak performance)
- Mental (rehearsal, imagery, visualisation)
- Strategic/compositional planning (structures, strategies and composition)

For example…*in badminton I wanted to develop the drop shot while improving my footwork (agility)…I trained in the activity using repetition drills to improve my drop shot…I also combined this with specific agility drills to improve my footwork.*

(d) **Whole performance improvements**

The response should include discussion and evaluative comments on how student's overall performance was improved.

It would be expected the student would give examples of improvements made as a result of training.

For example…*Working on my deep breathing helped me to stay calm and avoid distractions around the poolside before the race started. This helped me get a good start...the work I carried out on my tumble turn technique made my turn smoother, more powerful and shallower. This resulted in...the programme enabled me to...as a result my performance...*

3. (a) **Information gathering**

The response must show evidence of the importance of gathering evidence about the student's fitness.

Reference should be made to some of the following:
- Starting point for training
- Goal/target setting
- Needs are identified
- Comparisons before and after training possible
- Identifying strengths and weaknesses in relations to types of fitness required for activity
- Comparison with national norms

For example...I need to know what my base level of fitness was before I started training...this lets me identify my training load before I begin my programme.

(b) **Phases of training**

The response must show evidence of acquired knowledge of the phases of training. Reference must be made to each of the following phases:
- Pre season
- Competition
- Transition/close season

For example...before the hockey season starts I know I have to build up my aerobic fitness so that I have gained a sound base to then move onto more intense, competition phase...in the close season I would return to winding down, keeping my fitness ticking over by general swimming, cycling etc.

(c) **Phases of training – training programme**

The response must describe a relevant training programme for the selected phase of training. Reference should be made to some of the following methods of training:
- Continuous running
- Interval running
- Circuits
- Fartlek
- Conditioning
- Weights
- Relaxation, breathing and rehearsal

For example...in the pre season for football...I carried out a circuit 3 times a week...I did various sets of repetitions and exercises designed to build up my aerobic fitness...these included step ups, sit ups, shuttle runs, squat jumps...

In the competition phase I used plyometrics to build up the power in my legs for jumping to head the ball...I also worked on set plays such as corner kicks to allow me to practice jumping under pressure in a competition situation.

In post season I did some gentle cycling and swimming to allow some rest and recovery and keep my fitness ticking over...

(d) **Goal setting**

The response should show evidence of the factors considered when setting goals. The student should also provide examples of the goals they set. Reference should be made to the following:
- The point in the season
- Current level of performance
- Competition phases
- Appropriateness of chosen goals eg achievable and realistic
- The use of goals to enhance motivation
- The ability to monitor progress towards achieving goals
- Types of goals eg short or long term

For example...I set myself a short term goal for swimming was to improve my time for the 50metres front crawl over a period of a month by 1 second...this gave me a realistic target to work towards and motivated me to work hard and stay focused when training...another goal I set was to improve the strength for the arm action in the front crawl...this would enable me to have a more efficient pull through the water...leading to an improved time for my overall swim...this would be a long term target...

4. (a) **Mental aspects of fitness**

The response should focus on explaining the aspects of mental fitness. Reference should be made to some of the following:
- Level of arousal
- Mental rehearsal
- Managing emotions
- Visualisation
- Managing stress/pressure
- Concentration
- Determination
- Motivation

For example...in basketball as the ball carrier, I was able to handle the pressure my opponent put on me...I also was able to manage my emotions when my opponent appeared to foul me and the referee did not award a foul...this ensured I did not pick up a technical foul by reacting to this decision.

(b) **Skill and physical aspects of fitness**

The response should include detailed description of relevant aspects of physical and skill related aspects of fitness in relation to the selected activity. Reference may be made to the following:
- Physical
- Speed
- Strength
- Power
- Flexibility
- Cardio respiratory endurance
- Speed endurance
- LME

For example...high level of CRE allowed me to track and help out my defence as well as supporting attackers throughout the whole game...having good strength allowed me to jump and challenge for high balls and crosses.

Skill Related
- Reaction time
- Agility
- Balance
- Timing
- Coordination
- Movement anticipation

For example...in badminton, good agility allows me quick movement to reach the shuttle or change direction quickly...good timing enables me to connect with the shuttle in the correct place allowing me to execute the shot correctly.

(c) **Principles of training**

The response should show acquired knowledge of the principles of training considered when planning a fitness training programme. Reference should be made to the following:
- Specificity – activity, personal and aspect of fitness
- Overload – frequency, intensity and duration
- Progression
- Rest and recovery
- Reversibility
- Adaptation

For example…*I made sure the training was specific to the weakness identified…also to the demands of the activity…I trained 3 times per week with rest every other day…this allows my body to recover*

(d) Adaptation to training programme

The response must refer as to why changes were made to the student's training programme. Reference could be made to the following:

- To provide qualitative or quantitative details of the effectiveness of training programme
- To ensure progression and challenge while training
- Correct intensity of training programme
- To ensure motivation stays high while training
- To make sure short term goals are achieved
- To prevent boredom and provide variety
- To return to training after injury or absence from training

For example…*I applied overload after week 3 of my training programme…I did this by increasing the number of sets because I was finding my training too easy and knew I needed to keep forcing my body to adapt and get fitter…this prevented boredom and kept my motivation high.*

5. (a) Gathering information on Performance Strengths or Weaknesses

The response should focus on the information generated as a result of:

- Mechanical analysis
- Movement analysis
- Consideration of quality

For example…*when looking at my overhead clear using my PAR sheet (movement analysis), I could see at the preparation phase that I was turning side on…It became obvious to me that my weakness was at the action phase. I was not using a straight arm or hitting the shuttle when it was in front of my body. The transfer of weight was also not happening from my back foot to my front foot. At the recovery phase…*

(b) Appropriate methods of data collection

The response should focus on the appropriateness of the method described. Students must justify why the approach was appropriate. Reference should enable either qualitative or quantitative details of performance progress.

For example…*this provides evidence to compare progress/targets/improvements…a permanent record, can be used time and time again, aids motivation, and ensures further challenge and progress, information can be gathered at the beginning/middle and end etc. When using a video there is the opportunity to benefit from using the pause/rewind facility etc.*

(c) Course of action

The response should focus on the justification of the candidate's chosen course of action.

The response must indicate details of the considerations/critical debate about the selection and appropriateness of the materials of practice/development programme followed. In this respect the candidates should be convincing in their argument about **why** one method was selected in preference to another ie the 'process' should be obvious and justified.

The course of action followed should be detailed with reference to **some** of the following considerations:

- Stages of Learning
- Skill complexity
- Skill classification (open/closed)
- Model Performer
- Feedback
- Goal setting
- Methods of practice

Programme references may include actual description of the work carried out over a period of time.

For example…*As I was at the cognitive stage – I used many shadow/repetition practices to ensure – etc. At the associative stage I used some shadow/repetition practices progressing to combination drills…etc. At the automatic stage of learning I knew to use more pressure/problem solving drills as these would challenge me more…etc. I found the skill very difficult so decided to use gradual build up as this would…etc. In weeks 1 & 2, I concentrated more on simple drills…in weeks 3-4, I progressed to more complex drills such as…etc this built my confidence as I reached my target of…etc.*

(d) Feedback

The response should focus on the variety of types of feedback available when developing performance.
The student should comment on a combination of methods of feedback such as kinaesthetic, knowledge of results, knowledge of performance, verbal visual or written feedback when developing their performance. Responses must include the importance of using more than one type of feedback in the development process.

For example…*while developing my performance, I used my General observation schedule (written feedback) to identify the weakness in my game…this was useful as it…I then made use of the visual feedback from the video recording (visual feedback)…to see for myself where my volley was letting me down. By using different types of feedback I was able to get a full picture of my strengths and weaknesses, making my data collection more valid and reliable.*

6. (a) Features of a model performance

The response must explain the advantages of considering a model performance. Reference may be made to the following:

- Range of qualities – technical, physical, special and personal
- Example of high quality performance – few unforced errors, good decision making under pressure
- Comparison to own performance – strengths and weaknesses
- Motivation
- Confidence
- Goal setting
- Visual picture

For example…*I used the Model to help me first of all get a picture in my mind's eye of what I was aiming to do…this helped me set targets and stay motivated to work through my training programme.*

(b) Strengths and weaknesses

The response must refer to the student's strengths and weaknesses when applying their selected skill or technique. References could be made to the following:

- Preparation, action, recovery of skill
- Execution of skill
- Consistency in application of skill
- Qualities – technical, physical and practical
- Effectiveness of skill
- Mechanical principles – balance, centre of gravity, levers
- Fluency, control
- Timing

For example…*when performing the lay up in basketball, one of my weaknesses was the footwork… when executing the skill I often took off the wrong foot…this led to me being imbalanced…*

(c) **Principles of effective practices**

The response must show acquired knowledge of the Principles of effective practice. Reference should be made to some of the following:

- Setting clear objective
- Strengths and weaknesses consideration
- Awareness of model performer
- Achievable stages
- Effect of boredom and fatigue
- Intensity of practice
- Work rest ratio

Often the acronym S.M.A.R.T.E.R. features in the candidate's answers

For example…*practice should be specific, measurable, attainable, time related, exciting and regular.
…as my programme was specific it helped me to achieve success…I could target the specific part of my technique that need most improvement. I know to set targets and raise them once…this ensures my practice was motivating etc.*

(d) The response must give description of the method of practice used with relevant explanation as to it's appropriateness. The response offered will be wide ranging and will depend on the candidate's choice of skill/technique identified for development.

The response must include a description of an appropriate method of practice. These could include:

- Shadow practice
- Opposed/unopposed practice
- Gradual build up
- Whole part whole
- Drills
- Repetition
- Conditioned games
- Small sided games

For example…*in badminton I used conditioned games…I played against an opponent where I could win an extra point if I won the rally by using the smash*

The second response must indicate details of the considerations/critical debate about the selection and appropriateness of the methods of practice/development programme followed. In the respect the candidate should be convincing in their argument about why one method was selected in preference to another ie the 'process' should be obvious and justified.

Reference could be made to some of the following considerations:

- Stages of learning
- Skill complexity/skill classification
- Current Ability level
- Difficulty of practice

For example…*The stages of learning…as I was at the cognitive stage – I used many shadow/repetition practices to ensure that I was able to slow the movement down as I was wanting to get the foundations of the skill correct… at the associative stage I used some shadow/repetition practices progressing to combination drills…this made my work a bit more demanding and game like… at the automatic stage of learning I knew to use more pressure/problem solving drills as these would challenge me more…etc.*

7. (a) **Methods to gather information**

The response should focus on how information was gathered when applying the structure, strategy or composition (SSC). Reference must be made to the description of method(s) used to gather information on the effectiveness of the SSC.

These may include video-game analysis-observation schedules-knowledge of results-criteria checklists-statistics-personal reflection-feedback-internal/external-comparison to previous information gathered-match analysis sheets.

For example…*in basketball…we used a criteria checklist…all aspects of fast break…data was collected from a game this then allowed…comparison to previous…to see if we had improved its effectiveness.*

(b) **Recognising the need to maximise strengths within a structure, strategy or composition**

The response should focus on how the student made best use of their strengths when applying their SSC.
The answers may vary according to the Structure, Strategy or Composition selected. The following factors may be apparent in answers-to use particular players with particular roles-strengths of these players-type of opposition-attack/defence being applied by my team or opposition-time restrictions in game-after a particular time or situation in activity-ground/weather conditions-prior or previous knowledge of opponent/s-previous results.

For example…*When playing basketball we used the three tallest players we had to form the rebound triangle in our zone defence so we could collect rebounds defensively when our opposition missed their shots at the basket.*

(c) **Problems encountered**

The response should focus on problems which occurred when applying the selected SSC. The student must give a description of actual problems encountered.
The responses will be wide ranging and will depend on the choice of structure, strategy or composition selected.

For example…*in basketball we were playing a 2-1-2 zone…opposition had good outside shooters …scored frequently…and as a team we were not working together as a unit…this led to…*

(d) **Decisions taken to develop performance**

The response should focus on how the student justified the course of action taken to develop their performance. Response should show evidence of problem solving and decision making to make their performance more effective.

The candidate may decide to alter the structure, strategy or composition. For example…*in football we played a 4-4-2 formation…we found when attacking all 4 players in midfield would be up the park…supporting the forwards…when the attack broke down the opposition often broke quickly…our midfield were slow to get back…our defence was under pressure…we adapted the structure, strategy or composition by having one player…holding in midfield in front of back four…one midfield supporting strikers…and two in middle to move back and forward as necessary…this led to a more balanced attack and defence and allowed us to prevent the opposition breaking quickly. Holding midfield was able to delay attack…allows others to get back.*

The candidates may decide to follow a programme of work to develop their performance. For example…*in netball…the centre pass strategy was not effective because of ineffective dodging from the Wing Attack…we did some work on feinting without defenders…we gradually added passing…then passive defenders…then active defenders.*

8. (a) **Structure, strategy or composition**

The response must focus on two different SSCs. The candidate must describe **TWO** Structures, Strategy or Composition. Some will also make reference possibly to the role they played as well.

These may include:

Basketball-fast break…zones…1-3-1…horse shoe offence…man/man defence.

Football-4-2-4/4-3-3/3-5-2/3-5-1.

Badminton front-back-side-side.

Gymnastics particular sequence-routine.

Volleyball-Rotational setter, Specialist setter, W service reception formation.

Hockey penalty corner-passing it back to the 'injector' on the post.

For example…in tennis I used a serve volley strategy-I would serve fast and hard to opponent-follow my serve-get into net and position quickly-use a volley to win point-from opponents return.

In hockey…I played in a zone defence where I had to cover a particular area of the pitch.

(b) **The advantage of various SSCs**

The responses must focus on one of the selected SSC in part (a). The student must show evidence of the advantage of using this SSC.

For example…the advantage in football of using a 3-5-2 formation is that it is easier to dominate midfield…can cover wide areas of pitch…has a variety of attack options linking midfield and forwards.

(c) **The advantage of various SSCs**

The response must focus on one of the selected SSC in part (a). The student must show evidence of the advantage of using this SSC.

For example…My specialist setter can give me the type of set I prefer to be able to perform an effective spike…she can play a good set from even a poor first pass…giving my team the chance of more attacking plays.

(d) **Limitations of various SSCs**

The response must focus on ONE limitation of EACH of the selected SSCs.

For example…Limitations of a 3-5-2 in football is that the defence can be exposed…by long passes…played straight from defence…midfield can be bypassed.

Volleyball…the limitation of using a specialist setter is that there can be many rotational faults as people move too early before the service is taken or there is confusion in the front court as to who moves where and when.

Hey! I've done it

BrightRED
PUBLISHING

© 2011 SQA/Bright Red Publishing Ltd, All Rights Reserved
Published by Bright Red Publishing Ltd, 6 Stafford Street, Edinburgh, EH3 7AU
Tel: 0131 220 5804, Fax: 0131 220 6710, enquiries: sales@brightredpublishing.co.uk,
www.brightredpublishing.co.uk

Official SQA answers to 978-1-84948-223-3
2007-2011